He Whispered Life

Montessa M. Lee
I hope you find inspiration through the pages of this book!

Montessa M. Lee

xulon PRESS

He Whispered Life
by Montessa M. Lee

Printed in the United States of America.

ISBN 9781498441643

Some names and identifying details have been changed to protect the privacy of individuals.

Author photograph by Hollie Noble

www.xulonpress.com

This book is dedicated to grass-roots advocates and organizations fighting to bring hope, awareness, and change to those affected by lung cancer. Thank you for making a difference.

Table of Contents

Acknowledgments

I would not have been able to make it through my battle with cancer and pen this memoir without the support and encouragement of my friends and family. Your love for me gives me comfort and encouragement.

I would like to acknowledge my parents and my siblings for their continued support.

To my extended family of aunts, uncles, and cousins, thank you for your continued prayers and support.

Thank you to my second family at the First Baptist Church of Glenarden for reaching out to stand with me during my time of need. Your calls, cards, car rides, and prayers are not forgotten.

I would be remiss if I did not acknowledge my oncologist, Dr. John McKnight, as well as the additional medical team at the following hospitals: Washington Hospital Center and Providence Hospital.

Thank you, Dr. John McKnight, for never declaring a time line over my life and for simply asking me how I was feeling. My family and I appreciate you.

Deborah Leaner and Laura Jackson, you were there from the beginning when this book was scattered writings sitting on the shelf. Thank you for helping me develop my story into a manuscript.

I would like to thank the Free to Breathe staff for opening opportunities for me to advocate for lung-cancer patients and share my voice. Chris Draft, thank you for your determination to bring hope to the lung-cancer community by changing the face of lung cancer.

Last but not least, I would like to acknowledge the publishing staff at Xulon Press for walking with me through the publication process.

What Cancer Cannot Do

Cancer is so limited . . .

It cannot cripple love.

It cannot shatter hope.

It cannot corrode faith.

It cannot eat away peace.

It cannot destroy confidence.

It cannot kill friendship.

It cannot shut out memories.

It cannot silence courage.

It cannot reduce eternal life.

It cannot quench the Spirit.

—Author unknown

Prologue

Feed your faith and your fears will starve to death.

—Author unknown

Sometimes I can take myself back to that cold December night when I sat in the emergency room waiting for a prescription for painkillers so I could numb the agonizing pain of the machete that was constantly stabbing me in my chest. The pain had showed its ugly head earlier that evening and had virtually left me with no other option than to seek assistance in easing it. I sat there with my cousin Violet, hearing sounds of IV machines beeping, nurses pacing the floors, and my stomach rumbling with hunger. The unexpected trip to the hospital had interrupted my dinner. My slight impatience was intensified by my hunger. They had already done an X-ray and checked my heart. What was going on?

The doctor appeared and calmly spoke the words that would utterly alter life as I had known it: "We found a mass. We are admitting you." As quickly and as calmly as those eight words escaped from her mouth, I heard a jumbled string of words spoken so fast that my comprehension was halted to a degree: "tumor . . . IV . . . biopsy . . . possible cancer."

When I came to myself, a calm, still voice whispered words of assurance in my ear: "This will not kill you, but it will be a healing testimony for someone beyond yourself."

A battle had always raged in my mind that would leave me with thoughts of fear, doubt, and pessimistic thinking. In that moment when I heard the Lord's voice as clear as an alarm clock ringing in my ears, I felt assurance and confidence for the first time in my life; I was not consumed with fear. The relationship that I had developed with Him over the years helped me be assured He was Jehovah Rophe—the God who heals.

The Lord had captured my heart in the last few years. I had witnessed countless testimonies in my own life as well as in the lives of several friends. I saw how He had worked miracles for my church, how He provided the funds for the church to pay off the mortgage in record time. I had heard testimony after testimony from the church family, from saving loved ones to bringing others to His redemptive power. Surely He had something in store for me.

Although the road ahead was unknown to me, I knew without doubt that the Lord had gone before me and blazed the trail; He would be with me through this journey. I knew that I would be able to tell the story at a later time because it was going to be a healing testimony for someone beyond myself.

Part I
Prepare for the Unexpected

Nearly all the best things that came to me in life have been unexpected, unplanned by me.

—Carl Sandburg

1

Change

Man cannot discover new oceans unless he has the courage to lose sight of the shore.

—Andre Gide

It is so amazing how simple God's words are to comprehend, but often difficult to proclaim over our lives and to walk in faith. "The steps of a good man are ordered by the Lord, and He delights in his way," says Psalm 37:23. "For I know the thoughts I have toward you, says the Lord, thoughts of peace and not of evil, to give you a future and a hope" (Jeremiah 29:11). These powerful statements are so clear and simple, but I did not understand the truth of these declarations until I had to deal with loss and pain. Little did I know that out of my pit of grief, the Lord would sovereignly meet me at that crossroads in my life and relieve me from the decision of choosing which path I should take.

I grew up in a small military town in eastern North Carolina with my parents and four siblings. I am the second of five children, so I played the role of the middle child as well as that of an older sister. There was never a dull moment in our house. My friends loved the laughs and good times we had at my house, laughing as my younger brothers and sister often entertained us with their amusing antics.

The town was so small that we had only one high school. Some of the seniors who walked across the stage with me in high school had played with me during recess in elementary school. Even though several of my friends came and went through the years because of their fathers being stationed at military duty posts, my family and I remained in North Carolina and definitely referred to the state as home. I never even thought about moving away from my family and the home I had grown to love.

My family and I lived within a twenty-mile radius from my grandmother and the crystal coast of eastern North Carolina. We had the opportunity to walk around the corner from her house and enjoy all the things the waterfront offered, or we could travel the short distance to Atlantic Beach. We enjoyed the warm summer days by going crabbing, fishing, or boating, where we could escape the four walls of the house.

When I was younger, I loved spending time with my cousins at Great-Aunt Dot and Uncle Al's beach condo. We would stay up all night to catch a glimpse of the sunrise over the majestic ocean. Having the ability to watch the sun rise and set over the ocean was beautiful. The sun brought in the promise of a new day filled with new activities.

In the mornings, my cousins and I would spend time on the beach playing in the waves or swimming at the pool while Aunt Dot kept a watchful eye on us. For lunch and dinner, we would eat on the porch overlooking the ocean, laughing and watching beachgoers.

At night, we enjoyed walking on the beach, collecting seashells. I was amazed the first time I put an empty conch shell to my ear and magically heard the sound of the ocean, as if the waves were coming ashore. The night also brought the peacefulness of the breeze blowing off the ocean and the sounds of the waves crashing along the shore. It provided the perfect place to experience God's great creation.

When I went away to college, I desperately longed for the calm of the ocean and the opportunity to walk along the waterfront. I found myself surrounded by malls and the city, but I missed the unique laidback experience of life near the ocean. I did not realize how much I had taken for granted those picture-perfect moments of things as simple as a seagull resting on the post of the pier or a boat pulling into the dock, until they were somewhat out of reach.

Since my maternal grandmother lived so close, we spent a lot of time at her house, and she spent a lot of time at ours. As a matter of fact, she was the only babysitter I can remember coming over to keep an eye on us. When I was a teenager, I would often spend weekends with her. After I graduated from college, I would often visit her and ask her questions about what life had been like in her youth.

I can remember one occasion when my college roommate Vonnie and I called her to find out how to make gravy. She laughed but proceeded to stay on the phone with us to tell us step by step how to make the gravy. Despite her explicit instructions, our concoction did not come out quite right.

Through our conversations, I was blessed with the opportunity to learn about my great-grandparents, who unfortunately passed away before I had the opportunity to know them. In the back of my head, I never thought about my grandmother not being in my life. However, in the time span of a year, two events would collide and disrupt the comfortable, predictable life I had grown to know.

The domino effect started when my-then fiancé broke things off, and the wedding I was planning was called off within months of when it was supposed to take place. I was hurt, angry, and disappointed. We had been dating for six years, and I was emotionally devastated. God's divine sovereignty over my life was hard for me to comprehend at that time; the one thing I could see and feel was my pain and my confusion. I tried to move on and thought my answers lay in another young man I met, Myles.

As I was trying to recover from bitterness and despair, the unimaginable happened when I was awakened by a phone call I will never forget. I can still sense what I felt in that moment when the phone rang at six o'clock that Sunday morning in June. No one answered the phone because everyone was sleeping. We all heard the voice of Great-Aunt Barbara through the answering machine, saying, "Marie, Marie! Pick up the phone! I am at your mother's house with the rescue squad; I think she had a stroke." I could hear the sense of urgency in her voice.

Adrenaline immediately shot through my body, and I sat straight up in bed. I ran out of the room as I saw my parents rush out of the house to head for the hospital. Thoughts rushed through my mind as I stood numbly in the middle of our living room, looking at the closed door, perhaps believing the last few minutes could rewind in time. My brain swirled around me, telling me, "I was just with her yesterday; I just talked to her yesterday." Literally, my brother and I had been with her twenty-four hours prior to that moment. I would no longer be naïve to the fact that life really can change in an instant.

I paced the house, walking from the bedroom through the living room and then making my way back to the kitchen, anxiously waiting for the phone to ring. When the phone rang, I paused, took a breath, and answered it with a sense of nervous anticipation. My mother's voice greeted me on the other end: "Call your Aunt Deborah and Aunt Andrea and tell them your grandmother is in the hospital and that they think she had a stroke." I still had enough sense and awareness to respond with a simple "okay" before I heard a sense of urgency in her voice in her quick reply: "I have to go; the doctor is calling us."

I hung up the phone, breathing slowly and taking in the realness of the situation, but at the same time, I was silently wishing and hoping for the best. I called both of them to relay my mother's message. I told Aunt Deborah I would keep them posted after my mom called me back, but I was unable to reach Aunt Andrea at that time.

The time span is a blur now, but at some point, the phone rang again. When I answered the phone this time, it was the words I dreaded hearing. My mother was on the phone once again;

unfortunately, I did not hear the words I was waiting for. "Your grandmother just passed away," she said. "Call Deborah and Andrea, tell them what happened, and tell them to call me at your grandmother's house." I replied in a whisper of unbelief and my one-word phrase for the day: "Okay." I questioned why I was the one who was left to call and relay the message that still seemed unreal to me.

I called my Aunt Deborah and told her and my cousin the news. That was the first time I actually had to let the sentence escape from the realm of a thought in my head to speaking the dreaded words. "Grandma just died," I said.

"Montessa, what did you just say? What did you just say?" my aunt said in a loud voice, yelling and questioning me with a tone of disbelief. Speaking those words was what caused the reality of the situation to sink in. Suddenly I was living in reality, and I knew that I could not hit the rewind button. I had to repeat the sentence as grief took over my entire being and I could barely speak, but my aunt had to hear those words again before they would seem real. I heard my cousin scream in the background, "Grandma . . . what?" as I hung up the phone.

During those few moments, I decided the next person I called would not hear those words come out of my mouth. Perhaps I believed not speaking it would erase the reality of the situation;

vocalizing that sentence again would cause a flood of emotions I could not handle. I called my other aunt, who was out of town. When she answered the phone, I stuck to my vow. I simply told her, "You need to call Grandma's house." She asked, "Why?" but I just kept repeating, "Just call."

My youngest brother, Austin, walked into the living room as I was drying my tears quickly, and I decided I would not tell him what had happened. I decided I would let my parents tell him. Somehow I thought remaining silent would spare me the overwhelming sadness that was threatening to take over my emotions.

Later that day, I cried out, yelling at God and asking Him, "Why God? Why me? What are you doing?" The losses seemed overwhelming. At that time, I could not see the bigger picture. I had not grown enough in the Lord to know the promise of Romans 8:28: "All things work together for the good to those who love God, to those who are the called according to His purpose." I did not understand that the loss of my impending marriage was perhaps no loss at all and that the promise to believers was that my grandmother had left this earthy dwelling to pass from this life to the next. I was thinking selfishly; I was thinking that I just wanted her with me, not that she was rejoicing in heaven. When grief entered my mind, I had to put my emotions on a scale, weighing the possible outcomes: "She has passed on, but at least she didn't suffer.

I know she would not have wanted to be confined to the hospital for any length of time."

My beloved grandmother unexpectedly passed away on Sunday, June 30, 2002.

The funeral was scheduled for July 5. Since my grandmother was the matriarch of the family, an abundance of family members came to pay their respects to their beloved sister, mother, aunt, cousin, and friend. She meant so much to those whose lives she touched. I felt some sense of comfort and relief, having all of the family down; and after celebrating her life at her funeral service, I had a comforting message to ease my grief: "Blessed are those who mourn, for they shall be comforted" (Matthew 5:4). Life as I knew it was slowly changing before my eyes.

2

Open Doors

You will show me the way of life; in Your presence is fullness of joy; at Your right hand are pleasures forevermore.

—Psalm 16:11

My grandmother had lived in the family homestead. Generations of our family had been raised in that house, including my grandmother, her seven brothers and lone sister, as well as my mother and her three siblings (not to mention the number of relatives who stayed there at some point during their visits). We all had memories of gathering at that house to laugh with each other in times of rejoicing and to support one another during times of mourning.

One infamous story that was told involved a turtle and frantic calls for help. On one occasion, two of my cousins caught a turtle, and it bit one of their fingers and quickly pulled its head back into its shell, neglecting to release my cousin's finger as it retreated into its shell. My cousin was walking around frantically trying to get the turtle to let his finger loose.

My grandmother proceeded to call Aunt Andrea, and then she called another aunt, who worked at a pharmacy, trying to find answers for how to get the turtle to release my cousin's finger. Finally, she decided to call the police to come and get the turtle off. We laughed for days, imagining the turtle hanging from my cousin's finger while my grandmother was calling the rescue squad.

Who knew that out of that great loss, the Lord would open the door for me to walk down the career path He had chosen for me.

One evening the family gathered at Great-Aunt Barbara's house so the elders in the family could discuss what they were going to do with the family homestead. I was outside enjoying the warmth of the North Carolina sunshine and talking to my family members. I was talking to my cousin Patsy, a veteran kindergarten teacher, about teaching in Maryland. Almost as a joke, I asked her whether they provisionally hired individuals without a teaching certificate and helped aspiring teachers obtain their certification. I asked that question with a sense of doubt and unbelief, basically believing that the opportunity didn't exist and that there was no possible way I could move so far away from my comfort zone.

She replied, "I don't know; you have to ask my husband." I proceeded to ask her husband, Marcus, if they hired provisionally for special-education teachers in Maryland. I proceeded to tell him that I had experience working with children diagnosed with autism, and I already had a degree in psychology; also, I was currently taking classes to get another degree in special education. He smiled and said, "Come to my office Monday and we will hire you."

The next thing I knew, my cousin Stephen joined in the discussion and was saying that I could live with his mother, my Aunt Deborah, because he was going off to college. Every door was opening. I could not believe that something so painful could bring such an opportunity.

After I did some research about the county my cousin worked in, I discovered how big the school district was, and I quickly applied for a provisional teaching certificate. In North Carolina, I would have still been a teacher's assistant, and I would have had to finish a plan of study to earn another degree—all paid and funded by me. I knew this could be a divine opportunity for me, even though it would also mean a departure from my friends and family in North Carolina.

When Marcus told me to come to his office, I thought he was a principal and "his office" meant I was to report to a particular school. It ended up that he was in charge of one of the regions within the county as a whole. At that time, the county was broken into different regions or zones. Every door was opening, and it was beyond belief.

I went to Maryland on a Thursday and went to the Board of Education that Friday to fill out paperwork and interview with the human resources office. I had to leave Maryland by Saturday to get back home to North Carolina. When the human resources office found out that I was in town only for that weekend, they immediately sent me to three schools to interview. All three schools offered me a job, but I chose the first school I visited that weekend because they had the most experienced staff to help me walk out my new endeavor.

Also, the principal asked me a profound question during my interview: "What made you go into education?" I hesitated for a moment, and then I told her the truth: that I believed it was a calling as a result of an orchestrated series of events. She was impressed with my response and seemed eager to hire me. Later I discovered that the county was going to pay for me to continue my education to become a fully certified special educator.

Looking back, I know that it was only God. He aligned things at the right time in the right place to put me in the profession He chose for me. As an undergraduate student, I majored in psychology and did research with my professor, studying coping styles of children and families diagnosed with cancer. In my own mind and in my own plan, I wanted to go to graduate school to get a degree in clinical psychology and work with sick children and their families in the hospital. However, as much as I tried and as much effort as I threw into my own desires, the door was never completely open for me to pursue that path. Now I was seeing every door opening for me to go into the field of special education. It was definitely God leading me down the path of my destiny.

The first door had opened the previous year when I was filling in for my mother one day and helped her by substituting in a class at my younger siblings' elementary school. While I was there, I was talking to the secretary, telling her that I had just graduated and was looking for a job. The next day, the school called me and said, "We have a job, if you want it, as a one-on-one assistant for a student with special needs." Not having any clue what I was getting myself into and not knowing any details, I heard the word *job* and said, "Sure."

That student was an angel sent by God. He was a sweet, innocent child beginning his first year of school, and the Lord blessed me by providing an opportunity to work with him. I soaked up all the information I could from the three experienced teachers I was working with. The teachers taught me a lot, but nothing compared to what he taught me. He showed me how simple the world could be and how smiling and laughter could take you a long way.

On my desk at work, I keep a picture my former coworker/ mentor sent me of him at the Special Olympics. Whenever I have a hard day, I look at the picture so I will remember what led me to teach special education. With that initial opportunity, I walked through an open door to a new adventure with endless possibilities.

3

Transition

For the pathway that lies before me, only my heavenly Father knows. I'll trust Him to unfold the moments, Just as He unfolds a rose.

—Author unknown

I slowly adjusted to my new life in Maryland. Here I was, a small-town girl living outside the nation's capital. Myles's hometown was in the area of Maryland where I was relocating. We were anxiously waiting for the time when he would finish his stent in the military and relocate to Maryland. I was living in a semi-fantasy world, waiting for my knight in shining armor to come and join me in Maryland.

We were discussing marriage shortly into the relationship. Needless to say, I still was not healed from my previous relationship, and I had yet to fully acknowledge my emotional baggage. I was thinking selfishly about the benefits of marriage (mostly the financial aspects) and totally bypassing the significance of marriage, the covenant between the couple and God. From my state of brokenness from the dissolution of my previous relationship and my grandmother's death, I made unwise decisions. I decided to get married for all the wrong reasons, without considering any repercussions. Cause and effect meant nothing to me. At that time, I was living behind a mask of emotions that I had buried somewhere deep within that were waiting to erupt.

Through all of our discussions and half-thought-out plans, Myles and I decided to elope without even whispering a word of our plans to our parents, friends, or families. Seeing that I did not have the courage to seek my parents' guidance and approval showed that in the back of my mind, I was unsure of the major decision upon which I was embarking. Less than a year later, we were separated, and I was dealing with the guilt, anger, and shame of an impending divorce. That was the catalyst that really led me to deal with my hidden emotions; I had never realized that I was keeping myself a prisoner with my emotional baggage.

When Myles left one night after a heated argument, I was left in an apartment that I could not afford on my own, and I struggled financially. I was in a state of desperation, and I was falling into a hole I had dug. I went into a spiral of depression, questioning everything about my life and wondering how foolish I had been in my impulsive, selfish decision making. Even though anger and sadness overwhelmed me, I hid behind the mask and never told a soul what was truly going on behind the mask.

Somehow I stayed afloat until my lease was up on the apartment. At that time, I began another phase of healing. The Lord worked it out that I received an e-mail from a service ministry I was involved with from a church member named Nita, who was looking for a roommate. During the transition to moving in with Nita, my emotional healing began. Nita was also going through a separation and divorce, but she was further along in the healing process than I was. She encouraged me to take a divorce-and-separation class that the church offered. That is where my eyes were opened.

After completing a questionnaire that dealt with dealing with our feelings, I discovered that I was dealing with deep-rooted anger. That class was so eye-opening about interpersonal relationships and emotions stemming from divorce and separation. I really had to learn the power of forgiveness. Surprisingly, I realized that I had to let go of my pride and forgive myself. Over and over again, I was kicking myself about my decisions over the past year.

I grew spiritually, mentally, and emotionally during the time I lived with Nita. I thank God that He led me to her at a time I didn't even know what I needed. "You will show me the path of life; in Your presence is the fullness of joy; at Your right hand are pleasures forevermore" (Psalm 16:11). With emotional healing and spiritual growth, I could move forward.

4
Moving Forward

Brethren, I do not count myself to have apprehended; but one thing I do, forgetting those things which are behind and reaching forward to those things which are ahead.

—Philippians 3:13

My emotional healing opened opportunities for me to move forward and grow in my career as an educator and in my walk with the Lord. Professionally, I gained enough courage and confidence to step out in faith and apply to a master's program for autism and inclusion at Johns Hopkins University.

While I was growing and developing professionally, I was also pursuing my walk with God. I was encouraged to join a discipleship ministry called Queen Esther at my church. The name *Queen*

Esther refers to Queen Esther in the Bible. Through the book of Esther, we learn how a young Jewish woman from humble beginnings rose to the position of queen of Persia and eventually saved her people from annihilation. The story of Esther reveals the sovereignty of God over our lives.

Overall, the ministry challenged young women to grow closer to God. We memorized Scripture, had accountability partners, and were challenged to live as a light unto the world through our studies of not only Queen Esther, but also other prominent women in the Bible. In addition, I was able to establish some long-lasting friendships through the ministry.

I also ventured out in faith and had an opportunity to travel to Trelawny, Jamaica, on my first mission trip. In May of 2006, nineteen of us began the journey, unaware of the great things God would show us. What the Lord showed us was amazing. We were able to minister to girls in an orphanage, visit a local hospital, and nursing home. The Lord began to show me what I was capable of doing through Him. He led me to see His glory across the nations and to share the love of the Gospel.

The experience that I had working with the girls in the orphanage was a striking contrast to the students I taught in the States. A handful of the girls we met would have been considered special-needs students in the United States, and they would have been protected by laws that enabled them to have what we call in the world of special-education lingo and law "a free and appropriate public education in the least restrictive environment," meaning that teachers are required by law to provide an individualized education plan (IEP) for students with special needs to help the students receive an educational benefit in the least restrictive environment, leading to the inclusion of students with special needs in general-education settings. My heart hurt for these young girls. I felt like I was in a time warp back in the fifties or so in America before there was a wake-up call that initiated laws to protect and educate children with special needs.

The orphanage seemed to be a holding place for these girls. They were maintaining them to the best of their ability with rudimentary teaching techniques and resources. Small classrooms were set up at the orphanage (some of the girls did not attend a traditional school), but nothing was set up to meet the diverse needs of these girls. A burning question arose in my heart, asking what could be done to educate the staff about educating children with special needs. I wondered why the same laws that existed in the States did not mean anything in other parts of the world. America truly had its own benefits.

While we were in Jamaica, I was reminded of God's awesome creation. Nature shows that God is the same God everywhere, and He has given us this magnificent place called Earth for us to reign and rule over. From the majestic mountains covered in snow to the beautiful sun shining over the blue seas, God is the same God everywhere, and His glory reigns over all the earth.

I came back to the States with a new view of how many resources and opportunities we have in America. I came back with an overwhelming sense of gratitude. The majority of my students would never understand the meaning of not having any shoes to wear on a daily basis or not having the opportunity to attend school, and I would not have been able to grasp the reality of the situation if I had not witnessed it for myself. I longed and wished that everyone would have the opportunity to get out of his or her comfort zone and serve on a mission trip.

For the first time in my life, I realized how much I took things for granted and how many things I had wasted. Shortly after the trip, I heard the song "Grateful" by Hezekiah Walker for the first time. The words of that song resonated with me:

I am grateful for the things that you have done
I am grateful for the victories we've won
I could go on and on about your works
Because I'm grateful, grateful, so grateful
just to praise you, Lord
Flowing from my heart are the
issues of my heart is gratefulness.

I vowed to never complain about the simple problems in my life. That trip was the stepping-stone that invoked my passion to serve on the mission field. When the orientation came in the fall later that year, I signed up to go back to Jamaica and also to travel to Sierra Leone the following year in 2007. I was moving forward, drawing closer to God and developing a passion to serve on the mission field.

Everything seemed to be working in my favor. I was growing closer to God, and I vowed to submit my life to Him. For most of my life, I had searched for some purpose, meaning, and significance for my life here on this earth. When I read stories in the Bible about God divinely changing the name of Jacob to Israel, and when I came to an understanding of the significance of names, I set out on a mission to find the meaning of my name. Someone had given me a bookmark that said my name was derived from the French name *Montague*, meaning "sharp mountain." I discovered that my nickname, Tessa, meant "harvester" or "reaper."

"Mountain harvester/reaper? What in the world is that?" I wondered. I realized the reapers were the angels in the New Testament, and the harvesters played a vital role for the kingdom of God. I prayed that God would use my life for His glory and that I would be a harvester for the kingdom. I was excited at the possibilities that were ahead of me: mission trips, a stronger relationship with

God, growing friendships, and a growing career. My spiritual growth was preparing me for the trial I was about to encounter.

5

Dreams

Then, being divinely warned in a dream that they should not return to Herod, they departed for their own country another way.

—Matthew 2:12

Sometimes God sends His people dreams as warnings. I believe that was the case for me when I had two dreams that stirred my sleep and caused me to wake up in the middle of the night and record in a journal what I saw in the dream. I arose from those dreams with them still so vivid in my mind that I knew they meant something.

In the first dream, I dreamed I was on a porch or some sort of deck outside with an acquaintance from my church. We were sitting and fellowshipping together when hundreds of scorpions started emerging from the cracks in the deck. As they were swarming around our feet on the deck surrounding us, we immediately started stomping them with our feet. We were unharmed, but I woke up disturbed.

I researched what it could possibly mean to dream about scorpions. Initially I sought the Internet and started typing in "dreaming about scorpions" for answers. Then I decided to search for scorpions in my concordance and found Luke 10:19: "Behold, I give you the authority to trample on serpents and scorpions, and over all the power of the enemy, and nothing shall by any means hurt you."

I realized that even though things like serpents and scorpions were signs of darkness and demonic forces, the Lord had given us power over them. Also, the fact that we stomped the scorpions, let me know that the enemy was under my feet.

In the second dream, I saw myself in my bedroom, kneeling on the ground. There was a dark abstract force that looked similar to a cloud, pressing me down and hovering over my back. The force was powerful, and I literally felt like it was slowly killing me. Tears streamed down my face, but my voice and breath were being taken away from me.

In my mind, the only word that kept surfacing was *Jesus*. I tried to vocally whisper "Jesus" while the tears continued, but no sound would escape my lips. I was scared and wanted to call out for help, but it was almost as if life was being sucked out of me and I had no voice. Finally, I heard my voice break through and speak, "Jesus, Jesus." The force was taken away immediately, and I woke up, sitting up in bed with a gasp of air, questioning if what I had just experienced was real. I was comforted to know that when I called on the name of Jesus, He delivered me: "Then the seventy returned with joy, saying, 'Lord, even the demons are subject to us in your name'" (Luke 10:17).

I called different people I knew who had deep spiritual insight, seeking for them to interpret my dream like Daniel interpreted dreams. I wanted someone to clarify the dreams with the specifics of what they meant for my life. However, no one could give me the exact statements I was seeking. If I would have kept those dreams in the forefront of my memory and taken them as a warning, I might have been prepared for the series of events that were to happen in the latter part of 2006.

Part II
A Story of Grace

You are fairer than the sons of men; grace is poured upon Your lips; therefore God has blessed You forever.

—Psalm 45:2

6

Beginning of a Journey

Do not be afraid of tomorrow, for God is already there.

—Author unknown

I was sitting in my graduate-school class one Wednesday night in December of 2006. The pain in the left side of my chest was so intense that I was unaware of what was going on around me. It felt as if someone were stabbing me repeatedly with a machete in the upper left side of my chest. The pain had returned with a vengeance on my drive to class earlier that evening. My physical body was present, but mentally I was in a fog. I felt like I was in an episode of Charlie Brown with the Peanuts gang, sitting in the class but only hearing the teacher mutter things that were not decodable to my mind or ears. A classmate sitting next to me was talking to me about something, but I had no idea what she was saying; I just smiled and nodded my head. That was the longest two-hour class I have ever attended. Despite the pain, I was committed to stay until the class was over.

On my way home that night, my cell phone rang with a call I had been waiting for; it was my cousin Patsy telling me her daughter was in labor. Little did I know that God was going to bless our family with the miracle of a new life while I would be entering into a miraculous journey of my own. I called my cousin Violet on the way home that evening, asking her if she could take me to the emergency room when I got home from class. In my head, I was seeking relief from my pain with a simple prescription for painkiller medication.

By the time I arrived home, surprisingly the pain had subsided. However, I thought I could still use some painkillers. This trip to the emergency room would be the third time I had sought medical attention for issues related to this chest pain and shortness of breath in the past three months.

My cousin Violet drove me the short distance to the closest hospital. Boy, one thing I found out quickly that night was that if you want to be seen quickly in the ER, just say, "I have chest pain." Less than thirty minutes after being checked in, I was called to the back. I told them about the previous times I had sought medical attention during those past three months.

That September I had found myself in the urgent-care clinic with sharp chest pains that felt like a knife stabbing me sporadically; however, this night the pain had intensified. The doctor at the urgent-care clinic had poked around and asked me if it hurt when she poked my chest. Based on my responses, she determined I had chostochondritis, inflammation around the rib cage. I was sent home with a prescription for 800 milligrams of Motrin. The Motrin did the trick and eased the pain for the time being.

A month later in October, I had developed a cough and had shortness of breath. By then, I thought I had developed some form of asthma late in life, because I could not even walk the short distance from my car to the front of the school building without being out of breath. At that appointment, the doctor did an EKG and listened to my lungs. She heard a heart murmur that concerned her, but determined I had bronchitis and sent me home with antibiotics, an inhaler, and a script to have an echocardiogram to assess the heart murmur.

Based on the information I gave the ER, they predicted it was probably the inflammation again. They informed me that they were going to do an EKG. I must say, the medical profession was not sleeping on the fact that a young patient who appeared to be healthy could have heart problems. Thus began my routine of hearing "Remove your clothes from the waist up and put on this gown."

The technician came in, pushing a little machine on a cart. Then the technician proceeded to put several circular sticky tabs all over my chest. I heard the rules that I would hear several times throughout the year: "Now, be still." The doctors figured out what I could have already told them: the problem wasn't my heart. They said, "The EKG looks good. You probably pulled something; we are going to do an X-ray."

When I was waiting for my X-ray results, Violet and I sat in the holding room, listening to the hustle and bustle going on around us in the emergency room. The sounds of the IV machines beeping and the voices of the physicians and nurses conversing with their patients were masked by my own thoughts and my own agenda to be quickly discharged. The main thing I was thinking was that I was hungry, it was late, and I had to get home so I could make it to work in the morning.

The physician who was working on my case came in and said in a cool, calm voice the words that will forever ring in my ears and remain in my memory: "We found a mass in your chest. . . . We are admitting you; we are going to get an IV started, and perhaps we will do a biopsy. . . ." All I heard was "needle" and "cut"—two things I was deathly afraid of and was not expecting to hear.

Somehow the seriousness of the words "mass in your chest" meant nothing to me at that moment.

I proceeded to tell the physician what I was going to do and that *my* plans did not include any of her plans. My plans did not include any overnight stay in the hospital, and they definitely did not include needles or a biopsy. After all, my initial plan had been to go to the hospital to obtain some type of prescription to relieve the agonizing pain in my chest. Violet looked at me and stated very firmly, "You have a mass in your lung—you're staying."

The young physician had a look on her face that showed what she thought: that I must be out of my mind. I assume she came to the conclusion that I needed convincing, so she asked me, "Do you want to see the X-ray?" Still not wrapping my head around the reality of the situation, I had no idea what I expected to see on the X-ray, but we proceeded to follow the doctor to view it.

Violet and I could not believe our eyes when we saw my lungs on the screen. The best visual explanation of the picture that met our eyes was this: Imagine looking through binoculars on a clear night. You would see complete darkness and perhaps a few stars scattered in the sky. The physician showed me how the right side of my lungs looked correct by seeing the darkness. Now imagine taking tissue, balling it up, and cramming it in the left side of the binocular lens; your view from one side of the binoculars would be obscured with this mass from the tissue. That is what the left side of the X-ray looked like. Three-fourths of the left side of my lungs was covered by a cloudy mass. Only a small portion of darkness was visible on the X-ray.

After I saw the X-ray, the doctor continued to give predictions on what the mass could be, throwing out the word *cancer*. In those moments when possible diagnoses were being thrown out, I clearly heard the voice of the Lord whisper in my ear: "This is going to be something bad, but it won't kill you. This will be a healing testimony for someone beyond yourself."

By nature, my thoughts would have centered on worry and anxiety, but those were words of assurance that would go on to carry me through the journey ahead. Amazingly, through all the buzz that was surrounding me, my thoughts centered around notifying my principal that I was not going to come into work the next day.

Violet called one of my friends, Maya, and told her the situation. Within two hours, I had Maya, Chaunelle, and Katja (some of my closest coworkers and friends) by my side in the emergency room. Unbeknownst to me, after Violet contacted Maya, Maya proceeded to notify, not only our principal, but also our friends. I was surprised they came up there that night to see me. You see, the seriousness of the situation still had not sunk in.

I could see underlying concern behind their eyes, yet they were there to support me. They stayed with me in the ER that night while my cousin was handling some affairs for me and notifying our family. We were able to laugh and joke with each other about the things that kept us laughing at work and all the funny things our students said and did. In the midst of it all, Maya and I were thinking about eating, despite the fact that we were sitting in the ER.

One thing we all had in common was that we all knew the power of the Lord would prevail. I was touched to see that I was cared for. What a blessing it was to have sisters in Christ to encourage me from the beginning until the end of the journey. This journey would soon show me what true friendship, care, and concern meant.

Much later that evening, when I was settled in my sterile hospital room, I felt alone. It was the first time I had ever stayed in a hospital overnight, and in my mind, it was the first time I had ever considered myself a patient. I learned that a peaceful night's rest is not a prerequisite to an overnight stay in the hospital, because there were checkups in the wee hours of the morning.

At one point, the respiratory therapist came in with a breathing treatment. When he placed the mask on my face and delivered some type of breathing treatment, I realized how much my body was striving for oxygen. For the first time in months, my eyes began to close and my body relaxed so that I could fall asleep peacefully and easily. I had attributed my sleepless nights to my pillow or my bed not being comfortable, never that my body was being deprived of oxygen and I had a fifteen-centimeter mass sitting in the middle of my chest.

That night would turn into a three-day stay in the hospital. I survived the insertion of the IV, and I also endured the needle biopsy. In this procedure, an interventional radiologist did a biopsy by extracting tissue with a needle and the use of a CT scan to guide him visually versus cutting tissue from the tumor through an open-chest biopsy. I was anxious to taste freedom and desperately awaited my release from the hospital.

Once again I was less worried about my health and well-being and more worried about how I could afford all the hospital bills that would come after this stay. I was expressing my concerns to my mother on the phone one day when one of her coworkers, the teacher who had helped ignite my interest in special education, sent me a message saying, "Don't worry about it. Doctors love teachers' insurance." Those words gave me some sense of assurance that I would not drown in debt as a result of all the impending bills for the hospital stays, tests, biopsies, etc. Nonetheless, I still yearned to break free from the hospital.

I quickly figured out that I must be the talk around the water cooler at the hospital, because everyone who walked into my room asked how old I was. I almost thought of charging a fee for anyone who asked me that question. It was not until much later that I discovered that a fifteen-centimeter mass is an extremely large tumor.

My older brother Terence and my cousin Richmond came up from Virginia to visit me in the hospital. I was glad they actually were able to meet me on my release. Terence was beside himself and played up his big-brother role by escorting me to the grocery store to ensure I had everything I needed at home.

My Aunt Deborah and my mother were discussing plans about when she should make the trip from North Carolina to Maryland. The debate centered on her waiting for the official diagnosis or just traveling back and forth. I failed to speak my innermost desires: that I wanted my mother with me in Maryland. My aunt thought that it was best for her to wait for the diagnosis; unfortunately, I let my feelings take a backseat and never spoke my mind.

My dad called one night and simply asked, "How are you doing?" I have no idea why that sparked an emotional reaction from me, but I threw the cell phone across the floor and began crying uncontrollably. I yelled, "It's always about them!" I was referring to my younger siblings as being the reason my mother was not coming to Maryland that very instant. I put my face down into my bed and began kicking as if I were having a tantrum.

Somehow, Violet got the phone and talked with my father. He had no idea what he had even said to make me upset. He did not know it really wasn't anything he said, but it was what I failed to say that sent me over the edge. Violet was very nurturing and thankfully took me to the craft store to buy some things to keep me occupied.

My freedom lasted less than a week. When the phone rang one day later that week, I heard more words of uncertainty: "We did not get enough of a sample; we need you to come in for an open-chest biopsy." The less invasive CT-guided biopsy had been ineffective and inconclusive.

Unwillingly, I prepared for another hospital visit and my first major surgery. Fear was beginning to take over, but I had no other option. That surgery ended up with me staying another night in the hospital, except this time I had my mother by my side. Even though I was a grown woman, there was nothing more comforting than knowing my mother was sleeping in the room with me that night, and I felt safe. It took me back to my youth when I would wake up in the middle of the night scared and seek the security of my parents' bedroom. The funny thing was that no matter how hard I tried, my parents always caught me tiptoeing into their room with a blanket draped over my head as if I could sneak into their room unnoticed and invisible.

That would be the first of many nights we would share in the hospital together. This was just the beginning of the journey that was ahead of me. I did not know where the journey would take me or what roads I would have to cross, but I had the whispered words of life to carry me along the way.

7

Diagnosis

Cancer is a word, not a sentence.

—John Diamond

The surgeon who performed my open-chest biopsy called me after I was released to inform me that he had already set up an appointment with an oncologist. However, my family already knew they would obtain a referral from my cousin Keith, who was an interventional radiologist at a nearby hospital. We quickly sought his advice on making medical decisions from the beginning.

His initial reaction of telling my Aunt Deborah that she must have been mistaken when she relayed the doctor's words of "we found a fifteen-centimeter mass" should have given me a clue that a tumor of this size was not the norm. It was through Keith's recommendations that I found my oncologist as well as the rest of my medical team.

I was blessed to have a referral from Keith to see Dr. John McKnight, an experienced, thoughtful oncologist who was concerned about treating the whole patient. There was a consensus among various individuals who worked in various departments in the hospital that if they were ever diagnosed with cancer, Dr. McKnight would be the one they would choose as an oncologist. That gave my parents and me confidence that I was in good hands.

On December 21, 2006, I walked into the oncologist's office with another cousin, Stuart, who was lending a hand to help out. We finally heard the conclusive results for the mass that was invading my chest. Dr. McKnight said, "It really has a stupid name: small-cell lung cancer."

Since his statement seemed to be lighthearted, Stuart and I laughed and said, "Yeah, that is a stupid name." The same disease that had taken the lives of my maternal and paternal grandfathers was quickly invading my body.

Dr. McKnight continued with the conversation, which revolved around the next course of action: more tests, procedures, and another hospital stay. I was able to bargain with him to push my admittance back one day so that my mother and my Aunt Andrea could be back in town and come to the hospital with me. That night my cousin Bart, my Aunt Deborah, and I picked up my mother and my Aunt Andrea from the Amtrak station. I don't even know why I tagged along on the trip to go pick them up, because I barely had enough energy to walk through the bustling crowds at the station.

When I realized that I was facing a serious medical situation, I was advised to obtain a medical directive. I had to give authority to my parents to make any medical decisions for me if I was unable to make them for myself—questions revolving around things like life support, etc. For the first time in my life, I was faced with decisions about life and death.

On Friday, December 22, I slowly prepared myself to head back to the hospital to what I thought would be another short three-day stay. I was glad to see that they gave me a private room, when I arrived at the hospital. When the medical transporter came to move me to another area of the hospital to have some scans done, he was so funny and lighthearted. Since I was walking around the room in my street clothes, like a visitor, he laughed and asked, "Who's the patient?" Since I didn't verbally say anything, everyone pointed at me.

For a second, I felt special, being pushed around the hospital. My enthusiasm lasted only a short period. After enduring my first PET scan and capping the night of testing off with an MRI, I said to myself, "I can't take any more!" The purpose of the PET scan was to determine if the cancer was in any other area in my body. A PET scan is a 3D imaging test often used for the medical imaging of tumors or to explore the possibility of metastasis, the spread of cancer to other areas of the body.

At that time, it was hard for me to lie flat on my back. The pain intensified when I lay on my back, and worst of all, it was hard for me to breathe when I was flat on my back, which was something all those tests required. I remember experiencing the MRI and telling the technicians I could not finish the test because the pain was unbearable. Their remedy to ease my pain was to give me an injection of morphine. I was able to withstand the testing a little while longer, but the pain again became too much to endure. They had to give me another injection of morphine. From that first experience, I learned to dread both morphine and MRIs.

When I was wheeled back to my room after the test, I was starving, and all I wanted to do was eat. I had just started to eat my dinner when a nurse interrupted me when she came in to insert a PICC line. A PICC line was going to be inserted in the upper-tricep portion of my arm with the catheter running through my arm and to my chest to replace the IV and provide a path for the delivery of the life-saving chemotherapy drugs. The nurse set up her sterile area and asked everyone to leave.

Suddenly an intense feeling of heat overwhelmed my entire body, and as I was overtaken by nausea, I knew I was going to be sick to my stomach. I told the nurse, in an attempt to cry out for her to help, "I'm going to be sick!"

I realized my body was responding to the morphine. After the PICC line was inserted, my body was still rejecting the morphine. My clothes were so wet from sweat that was seeping out of my pores that I finally had to change into the hospital gown; at that point, I accepted the fact that I was truly the patient. I don't think I ever ate dinner that night.

In order for the nurses to start chemotherapy, they wanted the catheter to be pointed in a certain direction. They checked the direction of the catheter by doing an X-ray. I was praying that everything was good because I did not want to endure any additional procedures; it was bad enough that I was already trying to mentally prepare myself for chemotherapy. They came in and completed the X-ray. Much to my dismay, the catheter was not in the desired location to begin chemotherapy. The next day, I would have to meet with an interventional radiologist to see if they could reposition the PICC line.

The interventional radiologist told me that they were going to try to reposition the line with a minimally invasive method, and if that did not work, the worst-case scenario would be that they would possibly have to reinsert the catheter through my thigh up through my body. Thank God, plan A worked. They just injected some type of saline or fluid through the line and the problem was solved. In my mind, I was hoping for the best but mentally attempting to prepare for the worst. I was shocked but overjoyed when I realized my anxiety had lasted longer than the quick fix. When they rolled me out, my parents were pleased that they saw a smile come across my face for the first time that day.

My father; two of my younger siblings, Austin and Kayla; my Uncle Rodney, Aunt Andrea's better half; and my cousin Russell had all made the trip from North Carolina to visit me and pick up my Aunt Andrea. They were there to support me as well as support one another. Even though their trip was short, they were all in the room when the nurse began my first chemotherapy treatment.

So many things were happening during that weekend that some of the days seemed to blur together, but at some point, Dr. McKnight came into the room to discuss the possible side effects of chemotherapy. For each possible side effect, my mind had a resolution for combating it. Possible hair loss—That was okay. I had already determined that wigs were not for me— possibly scarves, but no wigs. Possible nausea—I was apprehensive about nausea because I knew I had a sensitive stomach, but his next statement was reassuring. He said that most of his patients did not suffer from nausea and vomiting, because of the antinausea medication he prescribed—another winner. Then he began to send out a warning of possible kidney damage as a result of one of the chemotherapy drugs I would be receiving, directives and steps to avoid kidney problems, and a mandate to stay hydrated. The last thing I wanted to do was end up back in the hospital with kidney failure, so I kept that bit of knowledge in the forefront of my mind.

That weekend I received my first round of chemotherapy. Initially I was a bit anxious and unsure of how I would respond. When the nurse came in and slowly began to tell me step by step what she was doing—"This is the fluids, and then I will start the chemo . . ."—somehow I swallowed some water the wrong way that choked me during her narrative. I felt like my breath was taken away once again as I began to cough uncontrollably and cry through my frustration. The nurse asked me, "Do you want your oxygen?" and all I could do was shake my head yes.

Something must have set the heart monitor off, because they called for an emergency code and everyone rushed into the room to do an EKG. When they came into the room, they asked the nurse in a humorous tone, "This is your emergency?" I guess I thought I was the doctor, because as soon as I heard the beeping, I told the nurse that something was wrong with the machine, not me. I believe the events in those few moments frightened my brother and sister, because my aunt and uncle took them to Keith's house.

Thankfully, Dr. McKnight also prescribed some medication that made me extremely drowsy. I did not have time to feel anxious; I was groggy and fighting to stay awake. Since it was a holiday, several family members and visitors came and visited that weekend, although I was so out of it from the pain medications and previous lack of sleep that I cannot begin to name all of them. I recall Dr. McKnight walking into the room and asking me how I was feeling. When I mumbled the simple response of "Groggy," his response was "Good."

On one occasion, I was so groggy I had a crazy dream that a medical transporter was pushing me through the hospital, but it felt like I was on a roller-coaster ride. I was being wheeled through a black tunnel with specks of light flying above and around me. Suddenly I was abruptly stopped, because it felt like I was being violently pushed through a set of doors. I awoke with a gasp of air and sat straight up in the bed. I quickly looked around the room to make sure my mother did not think I had gone insane.

It seems like so much happened in the short span of a weekend that year. I met the team of new doctors that would be treating me, all representing various specialties: a thoracic surgeon, a radiologist, a pulmonologist, and a cardiologist. I survived my first round of chemotherapy and had my "tattoos" placed to mark the area that would be radiated. Chemotherapy is a cancer treatment that uses drugs to stop the growth of cancer cells by killing them or stopping them from rapidly dividing, while radiation therapy uses radiation to kill cancer cells or keep them from growing. I would simultaneously endure both treatments, chemotherapy and radiation, for a period of time.

Through my meeting with the cardiologist, I found out that fluid was building up around my heart in my pericardial sac, the sac that surrounds the heart. In order to solve the problem, surgery was needed to perform a pericardial window. That meant they would cut a "window" in my pericardial sac to drain the fluid. In addition, they would surgically insert a mediport in the upper-left side of my chest, slightly below my collarbone. A mediport is a temporary medical device connected to a catheter placed under the skin for the purpose of administering chemotherapy. The mediport would replace the PICC line and be more convenient; it would allow chemotherapy to be administered through the port as well as provide access to draw blood samples.

Christmas Day came and went. One of my good friends, who was serving in the navy overseas in Japan, called me. She had no idea I was in the hospital and definitely had no idea I was dealing with cancer. She was a nurse who had served on the oncology ward, so I knew if I told her my status, her medical knowledge would cause her to worry. So I kept my secret until I knew my ordeal was over and she was back home in the States.

The day after Christmas, I was scheduled to have my surgery. I remember being awake when they wheeled me into the operating room. I was thinking to myself, "Why am I still awake? I don't want to see the OR."

The nurse was working on starting an IV while the surgeon was asking me about the pain medication he could prescribe after the surgery, because of my negative reaction to acetaminophen. The last thing I remember before going under was the circular bright light above the narrow OR table. I thought to myself, "Don't go towards the light." My mother told me that after the surgery, I spoke my mind, saying, "No more tests, No more pain." The anesthesia prevented me from hiding my true feelings behind a mask.

When I woke up the next morning and was lucid enough to absorb my surroundings, the drainage system for the fluid was not what I expected to see. There was a tube coming from my body. The tube emerged from the center of my body, slightly below my sternum. The tube was connected to a rectangular container collecting and measuring the built-up fluid that was surrounding my heart. I can remember lying in the bed the day after surgery. There were times I almost had a pity party for myself. I wanted to be able to take a shower and use the bathroom without lugging the container around that was connected to the tube emerging from my body. My plan was to sit in that room in the bed and feel discouraged and sorry for myself. All I could see was my present circumstance, not the fact that cancer was just a word and that my present circumstance of being in that hospital was just temporary.

8
Grace

When Jesus heard that, He said, "This sickness is not unto death, but for the glory of God, that the Son of God may be glorified through it."

—John 11:4

In my state of despair, as I looked out my hospital-room door into the hallway, I heard my mother come back into the room, laughing. Then I saw a lady in the hallway whose joy radiated into my room. She danced and sang outside my door near the nurses' station. I assumed this lady was at least in her sixties, and I saw she was not sitting around in bed feeling sorry for herself. She had a joy that could be felt by anyone she came in contact with. I can still hear the way she laughed that day—something I had not heard since my first hospital stay.

That day I met a lady who truly lived up to her name: Grace. By then, she had beautiful, soft, straight, short gray hair. She was beautiful and had a smile that welcomed all who came across her path. She brought laughter back into my life with her lighthearted attitude about her hospital stay.

When she saw the technicians coming in to give me another EKG, she told them with a funny sarcastic tone, "You'd better not come to my room next." She could relate to my reference to the tumor invading my chest as "my bully." You know, laughter can be the best medicine. Laughter reminded me that I was still alive and that "this to shall pass."

My mother and I also had the opportunity to meet Grace's daughters, and I realized that the saying "It's a small world" was true. Grace ended up being Katja's aunt, and I found out her daughters attended my church. Over the next few days, that "by chance" meeting led me to get up from my sickbed and walk down the hall. The nurses were glad to see me up and about and continued to encourage me to keep moving.

My mother and I would walk down the hall together. One of us would push the IV cart, and the other would hold the container that was still collecting the fluid. My family, church family, and friends continued to call and visit me to encourage not only me, but my mother as well.

One of my best childhood friends, Vonnie, was passing through town close to New Year's and gave me a call. Unfortunately, she had a cold at the time, and through her expertise and knowledge from a career in nursing, she knew she could not take a chance exposing me to any germs. I would later come to know how important it was for me to stay away from germs and large crowds where cold viruses could be lurking.

The days continued to pass, and the New Year came in with my mother and me giving a toast of Martinelli's sparkling cider as we waited for the ball drop to bring in 2007. The last place I had envisioned spending Christmas and celebrating the New Year was the hospital, but I was satisfied because my mother was by my side.

Normally, I was a person who was always on the go. Now, more than ever, I wanted to experience the things that I thought I was being robbed of because of the cancer that was invading my body. I was angry and disappointed that I would be robbed of my opportunity to go on the mission field that year. I was anxious about all the things I seemed to be missing.

However, after sitting still, I realized God was talking to me. He was keeping me still to whisper to me and spend time with me. In the regular hustle and bustle of everyday life, I had trouble hearing His voice. He was reminding me that He was Jehovah Rophe. He was reminding me why He had spoken to my friend

Nicole and to me, giving us proclamations of life. His grace was reigning over my life.

When my friends would come and visit, there were times I could not even get past the pain or nausea to read the Bible for myself, but they would read scriptures about healing to me. My church family came to sit with me and gave my mother a break, encouraging her to get out and about. She would have a short reprieve to walk outside and escape the atmosphere of the hospital. There were so many family members and friends who came in and out of my room, that the nurses mentioned it to Keith.

At night, I would listen to Stephen Hurd's song "Healed by the Power of His Word." Over and over again, I would listen to the words of the song until they penetrated my whole being: "I'm healed by the power of His Word. . . . Be healed by the power of His Word."

Volunteers would circle around the rooms on the cancer ward to keep us entertained. Sometimes they would bring around a cart with magazines or books; and one time some type of artist came by to do some crafts, but I was not feeling well enough to engage in any crafts. I saw that there were many kind people in the world who were willing to give one of the most important things a person can give—their time.

Even though it seemed as if my world was being turned upside down among all the chaos, one night I had the most uplifting, vivid dream. The dream was so real I thought I might have become delusional. I saw myself running through an open green pasture with tall blades of some kind of leafy grass, somewhat resembling a cornfield. All of a sudden, I stopped, and a bright light was shining all around me. I felt warmth and joy overcoming my entire being, and I began to smile and laugh. My clothes were changed into pure white linen. As I continued to run, I laughed as the breeze blew through me, my hair, and my clothes. I felt a sense of peace and joy as I fell down in the middle of the field, looking up to the sky. I was more reassured that everything was going to be okay.

> *And He said to me, "My grace is sufficient for you, for my strength is made perfect in weakness." Therefore most gladly I will rather boast in my infirmities, that the power of Christ may rest upon me. Therefore I take pleasure in my infirmities, in reproaches, in needs, in persecutions, in distresses, for Christ's sake. For when I am weak, then I am strong.*
>
> —2 Corinthians 12:9–10

9
Finding Peace

You will keep him in perfect peace, whose mind is stayed on You, because he trusts in You.

—Isaiah 26:3

On January 3, 2007, I was released from the hospital. Before my release, a social worker from the hospital came in to discuss all the resources offered by organizations like the American Cancer Society, such as transportation to chemotherapy appointments. She was asking me other questions, but I was focused on my release. After thirteen days held captive in the hospital, I came out assured of one thing: I never wanted to stay another night there, or in any other hospital, for that matter, and I was going to do everything in my power to keep myself on the outside of those four walls.

Soon I would experience the first major side effect from the chemotherapy—hair loss. Shortly after my release from the hospital, my large Afro was coming out in clumps. My mother helped me comb through my hair and collect the loss—so much of a loss that the hair filled a small office-sized trash can. My scalp was extremely dry and very tender. I gave my hairdresser Cammie a heads-up when we visited her so she could shave the scraggily remains of my hair completely off, meaning I was now bald. I was glad to see that my head had the perfect shape to go bald. Cammie was so understanding and supportive through the whole loss and even gave me suggestions of things I could use as a moisturizer for my scalp.

One day I found myself home in my bedroom alone, letting thoughts of uncertainty fill my mind. I was lying on the bed and becoming discouraged because once again I felt like the life I once knew was gone and the world around me was continuing to go on, and I was missing out. I got up from my sickbed and sought refuge through my bookshelf. I slowly ran my hand across the journals that contained the thoughts of the inner recesses of my heart. I had learned at a young age that it was cathartic for me to write in a journal. Through my pen, I was able to express my innermost thoughts and feelings that would have remained bottled up within me had I not found my voice through the pages of my journals.

Sometimes I would write letters to God, crying out for His comfort, or simple prayers, not only for myself, but also for other people; and then there were times I would just praise Him and thank Him for His wonderful acts. Other times I would use my imagination and dreams to create short stories.

Looking back at my life through the pages of my journals, I could see that the hand of God had been at work. He had guided me every step of the way. He had walked with me and directed my path in every aspect of my life, from choosing a career and comforting me in my sorrow to moving to a new location. I saw how the progression of my faith had developed through my praise and cries to God through my words. Here are some of those entries:

9/18/04

Dear God,

I thank You for Your blessings in spite of how much I have messed up in my life. I thank You for opening door after door for me. You have been after my heart for a while, and I thank You.

Love,

Your child Montessa

9/29/04

Dear God,

Today we studied the Shulamite woman. Lord, I want to have You in my heart like she had You in her heart. I want to have persistence and love like You have, Lord. I ask that You give me wisdom and discernment, for I do believe prayer changes things.

Love,

Montessa

11/7/04

Dear God,

Thank You for taking me to new levels of maturity and spirituality. Thanks for inviting me to fellowship with You.

Lord, I just want You to direct my path, to let me see where and what You are working on in my life. You know my waking up and my lying down.

Love,

Montessa

I was reminded that I was the one who had been asking for a deeper relationship with the Lord. Now that I had all my time to devote to Him, why was I still looking and searching for something else?

As I looked back through the journals, I saw how God had provided for all my needs during the time when I was going through the dissolution of my marriage. With an impending divorce, I was left with not only loneliness, regret, and self-criticism, but also with all the bills to pay alone. That, combined with some poor choices I had made, led me into a downward spiral of debt. I saw places where I had written down bills that I had to pay combined with late charges, praying that somehow, someway the Lord would deliver me from the stronghold of debt. I remembered times when I wasn't sure I would have enough gas to get to work, but through the grace and mercy of God, I made it through.

In the letters and prayers I penned to the Lord were the words and thoughts that I did not have the courage to verbally share with any other soul on earth. I had always been able to express myself more in writing because I knew that no one else would really have the opportunity to know what I was feeling and see what I considered my weaknesses and vulnerabilities. At times in the pages of pouring my heart out to God, I would use His words to encourage me. You see, I had to believe what He had already proclaimed over my life and how He had brought me through my previous trials.

9/13/04

Dear God,

I continue to be in a time of darkness in my life. People have noticed that I have been unpleasant at work. I just want You to renew my heart and let me have some rest so that I will have patience and endure the race at work.

As You know, there is something out of sync in my life. That is why everything seems to continue to go downhill. I have no idea what I am doing. I am going to order my steps in Your Word. I want to be in perfect alignment with You. Please take this worry away from me, for it is not of You.

Love,

Montessa

9/15/04

Dear God,

Please lead me in the direction that You would have me to go. I know Your will is not for me to be in constant turmoil.

Love,

Montessa

I could take myself back to those days when the only thing that prompted me to wake up in the morning and go to work was the students who needed me. Internally, I was in pain, yet to the world around me, I walked around as if everything was normal. Unfortunately, I believe my friends and family could see behind my mask. Thankfully, I had penned those words, lest I forget how the Lord had brought me through.

11/13/04

Dear God,

Thank You, God, for doing what only You can do. Thank You for loving me even when I did not love myself. Thank You for giving me life and letting me have it more abundantly. I will not let You down. Continue to guide me in Your Word. Thank You for listening and hearing my prayer.

Love,

Your daughter Montessa

12/5/04

Dear God,

I am sorry that I have leaned to You then left You. Thank You for never leaving me. I know You would not have brought me through all this to leave me now. I put my trust in You.

I shall not be afraid of ten thousands of people that set themselves against me all around. For You, oh Lord, are a shield for me. You are my glory and the lifter of my soul.

Your daughter,

Montessa

1/25/05

Lord,

Heal my brokenness. Cleanse me and make my soul rejoice in You always. I want to walk with You in all Your doings, Lord. Now having done all that I can do, I just want to stand on Your Word, Lord.

Love,

Montessa

8/2/05

Lord,

I have been broken (broken more than I need to be) to where I realize the only one I need is You. Change my will so that my will is Your will. Let me see Your will and purpose for everything. I have to be open to change. Thank You for loving me.

In Your service,

Montessa

Reading back through those pages brought back so many memories. I remembered those late nights when I had written those words in my journal—nights where I was plagued with bouts of insomnia because I couldn't turn my mind off and stop beating myself up for the poor choices I had made regarding my fly-by-night decision to get married and my now-looming divorce. Sometimes I think the hardest person to forgive is yourself.

I chose to walk down the path of marriage for all the wrong reasons. We eloped without the blessings of our parents and premarital counseling to prepare ourselves for a godly marriage. Every decision we make has consequences, whether for the good or the bad. My disobedience had left me with feelings of guilt and depression. I had to be reminded of God's promises: "There is therefore now no condemnation to those who are in Christ Jesus, who do not walk according to the flesh, but according to the Spirit" (Romans 8:1). If He had healed my state of depression, surely shrinking a tumor was nothing to Him. "He gives power to the weak, and to those who have no might He increases strength" (Isaiah 40:29).

10

Treatment

But Jesus turned around, and when He saw her He said, "Be of good cheer, daughter; your faith has made you well." And the woman was made well from that hour.

—Matthew 9:22

After I was released from the hospital, my mother and I were left with the question of who would provide rides for me to go to radiation and chemotherapy treatments. My treatment regimen was to be six to eight cycles of chemotherapy combined with twenty-two days of radiation. The slight glitch was that the radiation and chemotherapy treatments were going to be administered in two different hospitals.

Initially my Great-Aunt Dot rose to the occasion and volunteered to do everything. However, we did not want to burden her with the sole responsibility of transporting me between hospitals and appointments. It was during this time that I learned how much I was suffering from the bondage of pride. I had to swallow my pride and humble myself. I needed to open my mouth and seek assistance. When I surrendered and sought humility, the Lord gave me peace and rest. "Humble yourselves in the sight of the Lord, and He will lift you up" (James 4:10).

Reverend Gentry assured my mother and me that my rides to treatment would be taken care of. After the infusion center gave us a schedule for chemotherapy, one of my teammates from the mission team set up a schedule for every ride to and from my chemotherapy treatments. One of my friends from my Queen Esther group volunteered to take me to my radiation treatments on the days I had radiation and chemotherapy on the same day. My mother felt comfortable enough to travel home to North Carolina and make the trip back to Maryland every weekend I had chemotherapy.

I had no idea what to expect in having chemotherapy as an outpatient versus being an inpatient. There were three things I knew to expect for sure about the chemo schedule with volunteers lined up to assist me with transportation: (1) Some days I would have radiation treatment in the morning at one hospital and then travel to another hospital for chemotherapy treatments. (2) The chemo sessions would last about six hours. (3) I had a treatment calendar, and I soon learned the weekly and monthly patterns for my treatment. In week 1, there was blood work on Monday; Tuesday through Thursday overlapped with chemo days plus radiation (towards the beginning of my treatment plan); and Friday was a "fluid" day (no chemo, but I would receive fluids intravenously and also radiation). Weeks two and three were the same; they started with blood work and radiation on Monday, followed the rest of the week by radiation alone. I summed it all up by telling myself, "Okay, let's just say chemo week, blood work, blood work, chemo week."

I could not envision what the infusion center was going to look like. All I could do was to prepare to keep myself entertained for six hours. I prepared a bag with puzzle books, a Bible, books, and a journal. The precautions spoken by my oncologist were floating and circling in my brain: "Make sure you drink a lot of fluids; this chemotherapy can be hard on your kidneys. If you get a high fever, come back to the hospital; and call if you have any problems." I also remembered his warning about a patient who had not heeded his words and ended up in the hospital with kidney failure.

When I arrived at the infusion center, I quickly scoped out the place to see the setup. As I walked in, there were two chairs separated by a partition, with a large TV mounted to the wall in the corner of the room, and extra space. As I walked toward the back, there was open space with several chairs set up, with smaller individual televisions. It didn't take me long to decide I wanted to sit in the front so I could have space and not be surrounded by a lot of people.

If I recall, it was possibly my first day of chemotherapy as an outpatient, when I walked in not expecting to hear the greeting that my nurse met me with: "Okay, let's get ready for your blood transfusion."

Immediately fear rushed through my body, as well as anger. I said in a determined tone, "What? No one told me I had to have a transfusion. No, I don't want one."

Then my nurse basically told me that if I did not have the transfusion, they would not administer the chemotherapy. Once again I was overcome with emotion as thoughts raced through my mind: "Can transfusions be harmful? Why didn't anyone tell me so I could prepare myself? I don't want anyone else's blood!"

It seemed as if my sense of control and stability had been pulled from under my feet once again. Tears began to run down my face uncontrollably, and I thought as fast as I could and asked to use the phone to call my Aunt Deborah. I quickly dialed the number through my pain and confusion. When she answered, I quickly relayed the events that had arisen during those brief moments since

I had arrived for my appointment. She quickly tried to problem solve and come up with quick solutions, but inevitably she ended up with just giving me words of assurance that blood transfusions were safe.

Within a few minutes, she called back to relay a message from my Great-Aunt Dot, saying that her message to me was, "Your blood is bad, and you need new blood!" With these words of wisdom and some time to absorb my options (transfusion or no chemotherapy), I succumbed to my fears, dried my tears, and sat down in the chair to receive the gift of the donated life-giving blood I desperately needed.

Later I understood the reason why I needed the transfusion. My blood counts were too low for them to administer the chemotherapy. Low white-blood counts affected my immune system, while low red-blood-cell counts had their own side effects. I recalled when I was in the hospital and was freezing. My mother had to turn the heat up, even though no one else was cold. With the constant monitoring of my white-blood-cell counts and red-blood-cell counts, I sometimes had to get shots to keep my cell counts up. After the transfusion, I went home with a resolve to find every possible option to avoid having another transfusion.

I think it took a few cycles of chemo for me to observe and take in all that was going on with the setup of the chemo. The nurse would insert the needle into my mediport, hook up an IV with fluids and antinausea medication, and then come back later to hook up the chemotherapy. At some point, I noticed my nurse put on her gloves and securely pulled her facemask over her nose and mouth. I thought to myself, "Really? She is putting on all that, but what about my protection?" I realized how strong and possibly toxic the chemotherapy drugs were. After all, they were strong enough to target rapidly dividing cells in your body and make your hair fall out, as well as turn the tips of your fingernail beds dark. What else could they do?

My method to endure those long days at the infusion center was to get to know the nurses, the staff, and any patient I saw on a regular basis. I loved the staff at the hospital. They were so light-hearted and friendly. One of the pharmacists liked to joke with the receptionist. I was always privileged to be in the front of the infusion center close to the receptionist's desk, so I heard their laughter and jokes.

One day I decided I was going to revert to my joking ways, so I wore about a four-inch Afro wig to chemotherapy. The pharmacist laughed hysterically, held up his fist, and said, "I thought there was going to be a revolution," as if I were a member of the Black Panthers. Every time I saw him after that, he would reference the wig and I would throw up my fist.

I also met some patients that I was able to establish relationships with as we sat there and talked during our treatments. Unfortunately, I can't remember all of their names, but I still remember their stories. One gentleman I met, who was diagnosed with stomach cancer, would often be there with his wife. I told them I was a teacher, and they talked about their young child. He had had an "accidental" diagnosis, meaning they were treating him for something else when they found the cancer. He discussed the surgery he had gone through and some of the research about stomach cancer. He was already bald, but he joked and told me that he was hoping he would grow hair after chemotherapy. He indicated that he bought some big sunglasses to hide his eyebrows in case he lost those. He did not lose his eyebrows, but unfortunately, the hair on his head did not come back either. Eventually I did not see him anymore. I assumed his chemotherapy cycles were complete or the schedule changed. I still think about him and his family to this day, wondering where he is.

I also met a woman named Bonnie who came in with her mother. Her mother had come down from Las Vegas to support her daughter. My heart empathized with her the first time she walked into the infusion center. When she sat in the chair and the nurses began their questioning, tears were streaming down her face. She had been diagnosed with breast cancer and seemed to be in the midst of dealing with trying to have a normal life while at the same time fighting the war against cancer. She was at the beginning of her journey, while I was well into mine.

At some point during our conversation, I discovered that they were fellow believers deeply involved in ministry. They were already members of another church, but I invited them to my church and to come to our cancer-support ministry. Sometime after my treatment ended, I saw Bonnie in the hallway at my church. I found out she had brought her daughter to our "feed the hungry" ministry. Although Bonnie never came to our support ministry, she visited the church and chose to serve the Lord through one of the ministries.

I saw Bonnie again recently. I was serving at a ministry table in the foyer of our church. When we saw each other, all we could do was embrace. We looked at each other as if to embrace the miracle of life without saying anything. Tears streamed down her face, and a smile illuminated both of our faces.

Whenever I met someone who I thought was in my age range, I tried to seek him or her out to talk with in order to share our experiences. There was a man I met who seemed to be in his early thirties or late twenties. We were discussing our treatment plans, and he told me how he had to have his chemo injected throughout the day through some type of portable pump. He also discussed his fear of having children in the future and possibly passing on genes that would make them at risk to get cancer.

Another older gentleman I had a brief encounter with was sitting in the chair next to me one day at the infusion center, with his arm thrown over his stomach; the look on his face showed discomfort. Through the conversation I overheard between him and the nurse, I gathered that he did not have his antinausea medication because of medical-insurance issues. My heart cried out to him, and at that moment, I wished I could donate some of my medication to him. I realized I did not know what it was like to suffer through nausea because of not having access to the antinausea medication needed to prevent those side effects.

It was through my encounters with stories like his that my situation was put into perspective. I had to believe that no matter what I had to endure, there were others out there who were going through something more intense than what I was facing and had it worse, yet they continued to encourage me through their long-suffering and endurance to finish the race.

Radiation treatment was every weekday for a scheduled twenty-two days in total. Since radiation therapy started while I was an inpatient, I expected a transition period as a result of physically having to go to the hospital every day, but I was comfortable with my expectations. From the first radiation treatment, I learned that in order to get in and get out as quickly as possible, I had to lie as still as possible and take my mind to another place. When I lay down on the table and looked up, there were beautiful colored butterflies that met my gaze on the ceiling. I quickly determined how they manipulated the machine to radiate the targeted areas, so I would count the movements so I could target when the treatment would end. I anticipated what to expect as far as the physical experience of receiving my radiation treatments.

However, I did not anticipate some of the side effects from the treatments. The way the twenty-two days actually worked was that they split the time in half so they could radiate a smaller portion of my chest during the latter half of treatment in order to target a smaller field and avoid radiating good tissue as the tumor shrank. During the first half of the treatments, I came to a point where the pain to swallow was unbearable. I would lie on the sofa and wait for the pain medication to set in so that I could eat. There were two large dark circular areas—one on my back and one on my chest—that I had to lubricate with a cream recommended by the radiation nurses. It seemed like it took forever for the dark circles to go away, but eventually no remnants remained.

In addition to those physical side effects, the radiation treatment also could affect the red-blood-cell count. Since I had radiation treatment and chemotherapy together, it was hard for me to tell what exactly was causing my constant fatigue. I determined both of them were taking their own toll on my body.

I returned to the pages of my journal to express myself. However, this time my entries were short declarations to God thanking Him for my life, as well as tracking the journey and the miracle of healing.

1/10/07

I have to learn to not worry. I know that people are praying for me. Prayer is the best gift one can give.

Love,

Montessa

2/10/07

The greatest gift was given to me; I was able to spend time with my family. I realize how much I cherish and miss them. Thanks for the revelation, Lord.

Love,

Montessa

2/11/07

I have a family who cares about me, and the Lord has set me up with a family beyond a blood relationship. My FBCG family has been more than enough. My love for them goes beyond words.

2/13/07

The tumor is still shrinking! God has given me strength to surpass all of my human understanding.

Love,

Montessa

On February 22, 2007, my radiation treatment ended. When a patient's treatment ended, the radiation therapists and nurses all signed a certificate to congratulate the person on his or her completion of radiation. Whenever patients walked back into the waiting room where we changed clothes to get ready for radiation, holding that certificate with a smile on their face, we would all cheer for them and offer our congratulations. I was just waiting for my opportunity to be that patient. When I received my certificate, I was overjoyed with elation and smiles as I walked into the waiting area, holding my certificate over my head. I just knew that would be the last time I had to see that place as a patient receiving radiation therapy.

Radiation therapy was over, but I still had to complete the remaining chemotherapy cycles. In March of 2007, my PET scans started coming back clear, meaning there was no evidence of cancer in my body. It was good news, but the journey was not over. I knew that I still had more tests, more chemotherapy, and more doctor appointments.

It was close to my last chemotherapy cycle when my body felt like it could not endure any more. Fatigue had taken over my body and chopped my energy level from ten to zero. During a checkup with my oncologist, he asked me, as usual, how I was feeling. I answered honestly as I sat on the edge of the gurney, holding myself up with the strength of my arms, and told him, "I'm just tired." Fortunately, his response was not one I was expecting. He decided to push back my chemotherapy cycle, meaning I had a slight reprieve that allowed my body some recovery time.

I also told him about an annoying and painful ringing in my ears. At times, it was so bad I would place my hands over my ears and ball up on the sofa, hoping and praying it would go away. I did not know that hearing loss was also a possible side effect of one of the chemotherapy drugs I was receiving. Dr. McKnight sent me off with a referral to have my hearing checked, as well as a change in one of the chemotherapy drugs.

Since my treatment calendar changed, my transportation schedule to and from treatments had to change. I knew that some of my church members would not be available during one of the cycles because they would be attending a women's retreat with our women's ministry. So I had to ask one of my neighbors for a ride.

Ms. Peggy was another kind volunteer who had offered to help me in any way she could. I remember struggling to walk the short distance down the hallway to her apartment. I was just looking ahead, hoping her apartment would just appear, because I was so fatigued and low on strength and energy that it was taking every bit of my energy to walk the short distance from my apartment to her apartment. That short time off from chemotherapy was a godsend. I even started to get a little peach fuzz on my head.

Through it all, I chronicled my journey, claiming that my healing had already manifested. I wrote back to God the words that I had heard throughout my journey, not only to encourage myself, but also as an act of faith.

4/7/07

I have already been as sick as I'm going to be—I have embraced that truth!

4/14/07

Lord,

Please let me praise You. Let me thank You for letting me serve You. Thank You for being a healer and a provider. I've seen the mighty hand of God move over my life. You have taught me to take time and smell the roses. I have a passion to see the world. Thank You!

Love,

Montessa

By the end of April, I hit the end of my chemotherapy treatments and wrapped up with a follow-up with my oncologist. My Aunt Deborah came with me to the appointment to hear what Dr. McKnight had to say. He reported that the scans were clear and showed no evidence of cancer in my body. However, the next bit of news sent my mind into overdrive.

He told us that even though there was no evidence of cancer, part of the tumor was still in my chest. My aunt asked him what my prognosis was, and without putting an expiration date on my life, he said he could not say for sure at that moment, but if things continued in the direction they were going, it looked good. My mind was still fixated on the statement "Part of the tumor remains."

I assumed my aunt must have missed that small bit of information because she said, "Oh, this is the best news she has heard. She is so happy." I let her speak for me because I knew if I spoke, I would break down. Internally, I was filled with grief, anguish, and anger because I wanted no part of the tumor left in my body. My inner fears told me that the cells that remained could rejuvenate and begin to grow once again. My mind was infiltrated with thoughts that the cancer had a higher potential to come back with these dead cells still sitting in the center of my chest. I was holding in every emotion that would erupt if I spoke.

Then I had a glimmer of hope when Dr. McKnight told me he had consulted with the surgeon to assess if the remaining tumor was operable. He also told me that small-cell lung cancer was not usually treated surgically, but he wanted me to make an appointment with the surgeon anyway.

11

My Thorn

Once you choose hope, anything's possible.

—Christopher Reeve

I went into the meeting with the thoracic surgeon, holding on to hope. I was hoping that by some stroke of faith, the doctor would tell me he would perform the surgery and remove the remaining tumor. His news echoed what I had already been told, except that his detailed explanation also convinced me that it was better for me not to have the surgery. He showed me CT scans and explained that the location of my tumor was on my pulmonary vein, and if it was accidentally cut during surgery, I could die.

With that report, I had to succumb to the fact that the words the Lord had spoken to me in the beginning still remained true in the midst of the culmination of cells that remained in my chest. Later that night, I had time to really meditate and think about how I was going to handle this new bit of information. I recalled Paul's words in 2 Corinthians 12:7–10:

> And lest I should be exalted above measure by the abundance of revelations, a thorn in the flesh was given to me, a messenger of Satan to buffet me, lest I be exalted above measure. Concerning this thing I pleaded with the Lord three times that it might depart from me. And He said to me, "My grace is sufficient for you, for My strength is made perfect in your weakness." Therefore, most gladly I will boast in my infirmities, that the power of Christ may rest upon me. Therefore, I take pleasure in infirmities, in reproaches, in needs and persecutions, in distresses, for Christ's sake. For when I am weak, then I am strong.

I knew from the beginning that this was going to be a healing testimony for someone beyond myself. I had to recall those words of promise that God's Word was sufficient for me. I had to totally submit myself to the Lord and proclaim that my life was not my own. To top it off, the Lord had sustained me through this whole ordeal. Once again I heard the Lord speak to me with assurance: "Montessa, I didn't bring you through all this chemo, radiation, and surgery to leave you now." I just had to say "wow" to myself. Had I forgotten that I had been through all of that yet was still here on earth, waking up every day with the activity of my limbs?

When Dr. McKnight gave me the report that even though my body had no signs of cancer, part of the mass remained, fear once again took my thought life captive. In my desperation, I even considered asking for more chemotherapy sessions to rid my body of any evidence of the disease. Fear, doubt, and worry almost made me forget those words spoken to me by my almighty Physician that December night.

12

Am I There Yet?

After climbing a great hill, one only finds that there are more hills to climb.

—Nelson Mandela

Throughout my treatments, I continued my search for answers to explain my diagnosis and learn about new research for the treatment of this disease. Towards the end of my standard treatment with the radiation and chemotherapy cycles, I started to read research about prophylactic cranial brain radiation. Prophylactic cranial brain radiation is basically radiation to the brain to reduce the risk of the cancer spreading to the brain. Metastasis to the brain is common in lung-cancer patients. Research showed that patients diagnosed with small-cell lung cancer who responded to the standard first round of treatment had a better outcome for survival if they had the prophylactic brain radiation. After reading the research, questions floated through my mind: "Am I a candidate for this brain radiation? If so, I don't want it!"

I don't know what made me think I had received this information before my doctor did, but somehow I just knew he wasn't up on the latest research. I made up my mind that I was not even going to ask Dr. McKnight about the treatment unless he brought up the subject himself. Well, be careful what you wish for, because not long after my last chemo cycle, I had a checkup with Dr. McKnight. I knew what he was going to say even before he spoke the words "I want to talk to you about something." Immediately I anticipated the question he wanted to pose, so I saved him the time and said, "Prophylactic cranial brain radiation." He nodded his head yes, and I was on my way to schedule an appointment with my radiation oncologist.

In my head, I was going to hear what my radiation oncologist had to say, but I thought I still had the option to deny this new treatment plan. Through discussions with other cancer patients, I had heard how many of them had time to process their treatment options and make decisions based on the options. I thought this was my opportunity to opt out of any more treatment.

Part of me worried about the idea of brain radiation. I had already gone through "chemo brain," a term cancer survivors often use to describe the difficulties associated with memory loss and thinking difficulties after cancer treatment. My ability to multitask was diminished, as there were times when I became totally side-tracked and forgot to finish what I had started. For example, on one occasion, I was taking out the trash and talking on the phone, only to come back much later to discover I had never put a new trash bag back into the trash can.

When I met with Dr. Randolph, I decided to practice my "let me think about it" option. I asked her, "Would you go through with this radiation treatment?" She responded without delay and basically said, "Duh, yeah!" I kind of laughed to myself and realized that once again I was going to go through another round of radiation; this time my brain would undergo this new treatment.

Since I had survived the standard treatment plan, I knew a little more about what detailed questions I should ask. With the radiation being performed on my already baldhead, I asked if they were going to put the "tattoos" on my head. Blessedly, they said no. I surely did not want to walk around with marks all over my head.

Then fear overtook my body for a split second when I learned that seizures could be a possible side effect of brain radiation. Although the doctor told me that I would not be at high risk for that because of the lower dose of radiation, I was not convinced because I often suffered from headaches. I gladly accepted a prescription for steroids, unaware and not caring about the possible side effects they posed.

When I had walked out of the radiation clinic with my certificate of completion on February 22, 2007, I thought I knew for sure I would never again step foot into that place as a patient. Of course, I found out that I surely was not my own doctor, and I had no idea what future treatment options would be presented to me. At the time, it did not even occur to me that this new line of treatment was possibly a blessing in disguise. I was just ending my standard treatment plan, and my cancer had responded. As researchers had already determined, small-cell lung cancer usually responds well to the first round of treatment, but it usually comes back. Through research, they had found something that displayed success to increase survival rates.

The one fact I knew for sure was that the brain radiation was scheduled to last thirteen days. I could not envision in my mind how they were going to actually radiate my head. I soon had my question answered about the tattoos. They heated what appeared to be a yellow semiplastic mesh type of object with a hard blue outer band and pressed it down to make a mold of my face in order to make a mask. During treatments, the mask was placed over my face, and the outer edges of the mask were secured to the radiation table. The therapists put tape on the targeted radiation areas and put black Xs on the tape; I assumed those marks were my tattoos.

I used the same coping style to get through the brain radiation as I did to get through the earlier radiation treatments. I laughed and talked with the therapists and nurses and tried to converse with some of the other patients. When I lay down on the table, I vowed to be as still as possible, waited for the mask to slowly be placed on my face, closed my eyes, and once again counted the number of times the machine moved. I realized I was anticipating how quickly I could get off the table and get the radiation over with every time I would count the machine's movements.

My face broke out with terrible acne, and my face was fat and puffy. I did not realize it until I saw some pictures, but the top of my bald head was black. I lost the small amount of hair that had begun to sprout after chemotherapy, but this time I had a small patch of hair that remained at the nape of my neck, almost like a mullet hairstyle taking me back to the eighties. I attributed my acne and face puffiness to the steroids I was taking to counteract side effects from the brain radiation.

Throughout all my treatments, I found one thing very interesting: the treatment they were giving to save my life could possibly lead to serious side effects. For example, the first round of radiation could possibly lead to another cancer, and chemotherapy could lead to loss of hair, nausea, and unbelievable fatigue. Now I was faced with dealing with my own confidence and self-esteem because of my physical appearance. Nevertheless, when one of my doctors recommended that I should see a dermatologist, I refused because I did not want a prescription for any more medication to combat any more symptoms. I saw it as an unending cycle; a medication was prescribed to combat one issue but inevitably led to another issue. I could not subject my body to any more drugs or treatment options. I just wanted to start off fresh and purge my body of all the prescription drugs I had taken.

13

Back to Normal

O Lord my God, I cried out to you, and You healed me.

—Psalm 30:2

Initially I thought I would be able to return to work in May of 2007, but I was not cleared to return until the beginning of the next school year. I was out of work on sick leave for half of the school year. Prior to my illness, when I was able to go to work, I was always looking for a "snow day," but now I was excited that I *could* go to work. The Lord really took me to a place where all I could do was depend on Him and listen to His voice during that still, quiet time. I had to sit still, pray, and listen to His voice. I clearly heard, "Be still and know that I am God."

My coworkers were glad to see me return. I think they knew I was a walking miracle. I decided to wear a scarf the first day I saw the students so they would not ask any questions or have any worries upon seeing their teacher with a bald head. The scarf lasted only a day or so, and then I went back to my original boldness and walked around just as I was—bald. As a matter of fact, I received compliments from some random people who said, "Nice haircut" when a little peach fuzz grew back. My hair growth was a weekly topic of discussion among my friends. They were amazed at (1) seeing my hair grow back so quickly and (2) seeing the baby-fine, curly texture of the new growth. One of the first-grade students who asked me initially what happened to my hair would see me in the hallway, give me a thumbs-up, and say, "Looking good, Miss Lee!" when he saw that my hair was growing back.

The day I moved forward and stepped back into my life and career, I also completed my last day of the prophylactic cranial brain radiation. A simple word of declaration from a sermon I had heard earlier that year resonated with me as I came back to my life before cancer: "You've already been as sick as you're going to be." With that lone sentence spoken by my pastor, I was assured that I would never be back in the place I had just come out of. I saw the completion of chemotherapy, surgery, and radiation, but I could not see that the journey was still not over. Perhaps the bigger story was just beginning.

14
Lessons to Learn

Nothing that is worth knowing can be taught.

—Oscar Wilde

Prior to my diagnosis of cancer, I dreaded the thought of turning thirty. In my head, thirty was old, but when I turned twenty-nine in May of 2007 and Violet gave me a surprise birthday party, I was glad to celebrate another year of life. After my treatment ended, I knew my outlook on life would never be the same. I was able to wake up every morning and bless the Lord that I had breath in my body and was not in the hospital. I saw my life as a miracle given by the grace of God all by itself. Even though I was able to see and believe that I was a walking miracle, I was unprepared for the emotional struggles I would face.

I realized that while I was going through my treatments, I was just taking things day by day and fighting to keep myself out of the hospital. Somehow, someway I kept my sanity, and I was in my right mind. I did not even know how much I had endured until I talked to my friends and talked to other patients whose treatments vastly differed from my experience. I was going through the motions of the treatment plans, managing and monitoring the physical side effects from my treatments, but I never had time to deal with the emotional aspects of the cancer diagnosis. It seemed like everything started as a domino effect as I faced one issue after another.

Several months after my life resumed and I returned to work, my world was once again turned upside down by a phone call. Unexpectedly my cousin Violet called me one afternoon while I was staying after school late. The words I heard shook me to the core. The report was about Great-Aunt Dot: "They found cancer. They cannot do surgery; it's too far gone. She does not have long to live. . . ." I believe I spoke the word "okay" and asked a few questions, but when I hung up the phone, I was overwhelmed with a flood of thoughts that took over my mind. As tears uncontrollably streamed down my face, I just kept saying to myself, "No, it can't be. She was the one who wanted to take me to my treatments. She was the one who would take me out to eat after some of my treatments. It can't be true." She was the healthy one. I could not wrap my head around the events that were happening.

I was about to become an emotional wreck while sitting there in my classroom until my coworker's son ran past my door and stuck his head in to greet me with his jovial smile and wave. I knew I could not let him see me upset, so amazingly I wiped my tears and came back to reality. The next word I proclaimed was "It is not true. God healed me, and He will heal Aunt Dot."

8/8/08

Lord,

I thank You for being all that You are. I thank You for being a healer and a redeemer. I thank You for letting me walk in Your Word. Wash me whiter than snow.

God, I want You to curse the root of the enemy. You gave us power over scorpions and things of the world. We can trample on the enemy. I curse the root of cancer. Father, send it away. When Dorothy Horton goes for testing, I bind the hand of the enemy that says cancer. Don't even let the words escape from their lips. Let the prayers of the righteous go forth. Let no one else in my family come down with cancer.

You said that we are healed by Your stripes. You said the Sun of Righteousness would rise with healing in His wings. We overcome the enemy by the blood of the Lamb and by the words of our testimonies. Healing, Jesus! Thank You for all You have done and all You will do. Show Yourself strong.

Montessa

Sooner than later, the doctor's words prevailed, and we lost another matriarch of our family. I was angry and did not understand why her life was taken from us. The word *cancer* disgusted me, and I questioned why she was not healed. She herself was a fighter, and she had told me, "I know you know that they found these tumors, but I'm going to fight it."

It took me a while to come to grips with the truth: that even though I was grieving, she had lived a long, prosperous life and touched many lives along the way. Her life was over on this earth, but she would live on forever in my heart. "For we know that if our earthly house, this tent, is destroyed, we have a building from God, a house not made with hands, eternal in the heavens" (2 Corinthians 5:1). I was able to come to some level of reasoning dealing with that loss, but some of the other things I faced were not as easy to deal with.

In the midst of trying to reestablish my life, the Lord opened the door for me to fulfill my passion to carry out the Great Commission and go back on the mission field. While I thought my opportunities to travel to the ends of the earth were gone since I had been out of commission for a while, I had no idea that the Lord had more in store than I could have ever imagined. He took me beyond my level of thinking and took me not only on another trip to Jamaica, but also on a new adventure to Bangkok, Thailand.

In Thailand, I was able to share my testimony of healing with the people. The Lord continued to speak through me when the students we were teaching English to asked me questions that were challenges to my declaration of faith. One young lady stood up and curiously asked, "How do you *know* the Lord was with you?" Knowing that I had been given this prime opportunity to share the loving power of the Gospel, I smiled as the Lord spoke through me to respond to her question. I was also able to tell her how He had walked with me every step of the way. I believe that night was the first night I was able to verbally speak the words I already knew were true: "God left me alive for a reason, and my life is not my own." Scripture had truly come alive for me: "And they overcame him by the blood of the Lamb and by the word of their testimony, and they did not love their lives to the death" (Revelation 12:11). My spirit and mind were opened to see how the words of my testimony were coming alive for someone beyond me, thousands of miles from what I called home.

Unfortunately, my high after returning to the States was quickly deflated. I was checking my e-mail after my return from Thailand when I read the messages from my cancer-support ministry. The words were a blur, but I was able to see those key words that caused me to scan the message several times: "We regret to inform you of the passing of Dee. . . . Funeral arrangements are . . . The second message said, "We regret to inform you of our brother's passing. Funeral arrangements for Kimothy will be . . ."

Immediately thoughts raced through my head as I asked "what?" and realized that I had not even been around to pay my respects. These were two more people I had lost to cancer—this disease that could cripple one's life in a matter of months. I was overwhelmed with emotion once again, not knowing if this would be a continuous cycle I would have to face over and over again.

Dee was one of the first people I had met when I joined the cancer-support ministry. She was always smiling as she went through her battle with ovarian cancer. Her strength and perseverance encouraged me as I saw her smile at every meeting and as she would call me and try to plan opportunities to reach out and visit other members in our support ministry who were hospitalized. Her mother often attended our meetings and walked the long journey with her daughter. I knew Dee had younger children, and they had also recently lost their father. I grieved for the children.

I knew Kimothy's wife from another ministry. He also had been diagnosed with lung cancer, so we shared a bond. He left behind a wife and children. My emotions saw these children, caregivers, and families who had lost their mother, father, husband, or daughter, and I personally came to understand what the term *survivor's guilt* felt like.

The concept of survivor's guilt was always hard for me to wrap my head around until I had firsthand experience. I began to struggle with why I was still walking on the face of this earth while these others were taken away. I yelled to God through my tears, "Why did they have to die? It's not fair; they have a family with children!" In that split second, I forgot that the Lord I served was a sovereign God and that as He had spoken to me earlier, my purpose in this world was not finished. After some period of struggling with my grief and questioning of God, I was once again able to see the larger picture.

I was disturbed because I had not been in the States to get the message at the time the news went out. Later I thought about it and knew it was God's divine intervention. He knew what I could handle, for He will never give us more than we can endure. I was at the place I was destined to be at that moment in time.

In our cancer-support ministry, when possible we paired up with people who had been diagnosed with the same cancer in order to support one another through firsthand understanding. There were only a couple of times individuals came to the ministry with a lung-cancer diagnosis. On one occasion, I met one older lady who had been diagnosed with lung cancer. As Dee and I had discussed, when I found out she was in the hospital, I went to visit her.

I do not know what possessed me to think I could handle seeing someone in the place I had just come from. As soon as I walked through the doors of the hospital and walked down the hall to her room, a flood of emotions overtook me. I became tense and thought about turning around. Somehow I made it to her room, but my brain seemed to have lost the ability to connect to my mouth and produce words. I was able to utter a small greeting to her as I sat in a chair across from her hospital bed.

Suddenly visions infiltrated my head, bringing me back to the time when I was in her place. I saw the oxygen tubes extending from her nose, and I remembered when my body was in desperate need of air. I saw the IV connected to her, injecting either life-saving medicine or fluids into her body. The beeping of the IV machine and the neighbor lying in the bed next to her brought back a flood of memories I did not want to relive.

In my mind, I was trying to think of a rational reason to flee. A nurse came in to do something and gave me my opportunity to escape. I realized that it hit too close to home at that moment in my life for me to visit the sick in the hospital; I hoped that would not always be the case.

New research is being conducted in the area of cancer survivorship; that is, patients living with the disease and patients after treatment ends, as well as looking at how the disease affects caregivers, friends, and family. It's amazing how many aspects of life cancer survivors and their caregivers can face, especially the whole realm of emotional issues.

After the treatments ended, I went through a "divorce" with my team of health-care providers. When you are used to seeing the same friendly faces week after week through the most challenging time in your life, you are left with the question of "what do I do now?" Every time I had a cough or slight pain, fear threatened to take over my mind: "Has the cancer come back? Am I getting a cold?" I had to visit the infusion center once a month for a quick visit to have my mediport flushed, but it wasn't the same. My frequent visits had become a quick passing through. My new treatment plan consisted of visiting the oncologist about every four months and eventually dwindling down to annual visits. At that time, I felt like I was missing the caregivers I had established relationships with over the time I was going through treatment.

After growing up and babysitting three younger siblings at times, I thought I never wanted to have children. When people asked me if I had any children, I would answer no but refer to the many children I taught as being enough. It's funny that when I learned the chemotherapy could affect my fertility, my beliefs shifted. Once again I saw the chemotherapy treatments as possibly robbing me of something: that even if I desired to have children, there was a chance that the chemo had annihilated that possibility.

Even though I had fought the good fight and remained strong, my confidence and self-esteem had been shaken. I had learned what a good friend was through this ordeal: "A man who has friends must himself be friendly, but there is a friend who sticks closer than a brother" (Proverbs 18:24). That knowledge also gave me a deep understanding of the people I wanted surrounding me in my life. I had thoughts that no man would ever want to marry me, knowing he would have to deal with the chance that the cancer might return or that there was a possibility that I would never be able to bear children. Unfortunately, once again I was letting thoughts of doubt, worry, and fear infiltrate my mind.

The Lord continued to send people into my life to encourage me, and He also spoke to me through the promise of His Word. I once again poured out my heart and soul through penned messages to the only one who could give me peace.

2/1/2008

"And they overcame him by the blood of the Lamb and by the power of their testimonies." Thank You for letting us win the battle. I have enjoyed the fight, because through it, You have shown me so much. Lord, speak Your purpose for my life. Show me how You want me to get the word out and reach people about lung cancer in young nonsmokers and about an increased level of research. Open doors for me, Lord, and speak to me, Lord.

Love,

Montessa

That powerful scripture would become a life scripture for me because of my personal testimony: "And they *overcame* him *by the blood of the Lamb* and by the word of their testimony, and they did not love their lives to death" (Revelation 12:11, emphasis added). I had the victory through the blood of Jesus!

2/8/08

You have given me a blessing. Truly the hand of God is on my life. You are looking at a miracle. . . . In all that I went through, I remembered the voice saying, "This will not kill you!"

2/23/08

Lord,

Please let me express that You are the great Jehovah Jireh, the great Jehovah Rophe. You are awesome, Lord! I confess that my thoughts are often not Your thoughts, and my ways are often not Your ways, but thank You for Your grace and mercy.

Love,

Montessa

Though I felt like I was riding on an emotional roller coaster at times, I had to proclaim what God had already spoken. I combated the fear of the cancer returning with the words of the prophet Isaiah: "Surely He has borne our griefs and carried our sorrows; yet we esteemed Him stricken, smitten by God, and afflicted. But He was wounded for our transgressions, He was bruised for our iniquities; the chastisement of peace was upon Him, and by His stripes we are *healed*" (Isaiah 53:4–5, emphasis added). "Montessa, by His stripes you are healed!" I proclaimed.

My mind had to occasionally be reminded of the calming voice of peace and assurance spoken to me at the beginning of this journey and the single isolated statement spoken in a message from my pastor that resonated in my spirit: "You've already been as sick as you're going to be." Never again would I be confined to a hospital bed, dealing with cancer.

Like a weary traveler asks the question, "Are we there yet?" I knew that the answer was no. God was teaching me how to lean on faith and be assured that He knew the plans He had for me. In my analytical mind, I wanted to be prepared for what was to come. I wanted to be prepared if I came to another fork in the road as I continued traveling this unpredictable road. Comfort and assurance came through His Word: "And the Lord, He is the One who goes before you. He will be with you, He will not leave you nor forsake you; do not fear nor be dismayed" (Deuteronomy 31:8). Whatever the Lord had for me, He had already prepared the way; wherever He was taking me, He would be with me every step of the way. What a blessed assurance that all I had to do was walk in it and believe what He said.

I proclaimed victory over my life, over the powers of darkness, and left as the signature line on my e-mail Revelation 12:11: "And they overcame him with the blood of the Lamb and by the word of their testimony, and they did not love their lives to the death." I knew that somehow, someway my testimony would make a difference in the life of someone else. The story wasn't for me alone.

Even though I did not find my niche through visiting people in the hospital at that moment in my journey, a compelling passion stirred in my spirit to pray for healing and peace for others who were battling cancer. I had an army of prayer warriors sending up prayers on my behalf and keeping me encouraged through cards, letters, visits, and phone calls. I committed myself to call out before God the names of other people who were facing trials in their lives. My heart was burdened to pray for those individuals and return what had been given to me when I was going through treatment. I began to send cards with words of encouragement to keep others marching on toward victory.

Part III
Identify Yourself

To live is the rarest thing in the world. Most people exist, that is all.

—Oscar Wilde

15

Fighting Back

Never doubt that a small group of committed people can change the world. Indeed, it is the only thing that ever has.

—Margaret Mead

Initially, when I received the diagnosis of lung cancer, I went on a desperate search to find the origin of this disease that had invaded my body, because I was a nonsmoker and also had not been exposed to secondhand smoke. I thought I may have been exposed to asbestos at work and called environmental people, reaching out for an answer. My Aunt Dot found out that families who had lived on a military base near the town I grew up in were involved in lawsuits because of increased cancer rates. She wanted me to research the findings and join the lawsuit if possible. She thought that I might have been exposed to some kind of environmental hazard and was disappointed that I had suffered two misdiagnoses. Everyone wondered if the situation would have been different if the cancer had been detected earlier.

During my exploration phase to find answers, I tried to enter a genetic study examining lung cancer in individuals who had never smoked, but I was disqualified from that study because of the fact that they were exclusively studying non–small-cell lung cancer, not small-cell lung cancer. At some point, I had to come to grips with the fact that I might never discover how this disease had taken root in my body and that my increased focus to seek answers would eventually wear me down. I also realized that a lawsuit meant nothing. Money would solve nothing; money could not ease emotional pain. I knew that my goal would be much different and hopefully make a larger impact.

That December night when the physicians ordered an X-ray and found the fifteen-centimeter mass, they apologized that no one had ever given me an X-ray prior to that night in the emergency room. The doctor said, "If you were sixty with the same symptoms, they would have automatically given you an X-ray." I knew that my diagnosis could possibly open the eyes of the physicians to not sleep on other young, apparently healthy patients who came in with similar symptoms. Young nonsmokers with a healthy lifestyle could still be diagnosed with lung cancer.

In the midst of searching for answers and clarification about my diagnosis of small-cell lung cancer, I did not find hope for a positive outlook, and I found that most of us would not live long enough to be considered a five-year survivor. Lung cancer is usually broken down into two large categories: non–small-cell lung cancer, with four smaller subcategories; and small-cell lung cancer, making up a smaller percentage of patients diagnosed with lung cancer. Not only was my diagnosis in the smaller percentage of lung-cancer diagnoses, but also I was diagnosed with the more aggressive form of lung cancer. Statistics revealed that the five-year survival rate for lung cancer was a mere 16 percent and that 160,000 people died each year from lung cancer. I thanked God that He gave me a word of healing before I learned the seriousness of the disease.

Although lung cancer kills more people than prostate, colon, and breast cancers combined, there is startling disparity in the dispersion of research funds to individual cancer sites. Anger emerged as I saw that the survival rates for lung cancer had not increased much over the years. We were in desperate need of an effective prescreening test to detect early- stage lung cancer. Mammograms exist for breast-cancer detection, and colonoscopies exist to detect colon cancer, but what hope did we have for early detection of lung cancer?

One factor leading to the low survival rates was that lung cancer was often detected after it had metastasized. This same disease had taken my maternal and paternal grandfathers' lives before I really got to know them, years before my diagnosis. But generations later, the numbers basically said that I would suffer the same fate that they did.

I turned my anger into passion and commitment to help make lung cancer a national priority and to raise public awareness of this deadly disease. I have hope that public awareness and increases in research can halt the 160,000 deaths a year that result from lung cancer. I saw that the tobacco-cessation programs had been effective in their efforts to curb smoking. (Smoking is often associated with lung cancer as well as with other diseases.) However, it seemed to also attach a huge price for lung-cancer patients—*stigma*.

The first question people often ask lung cancer patients is "Did you smoke?" I felt the lung-cancer community somehow had to move past this stigma and educate the public if we were ever going to see improved research for the disease. I did not even know where to begin, so I signed up for information on any lung-cancer advocacy movement I found on the Internet.

After I participated in movements via signing petitions to pass acts like the Lung Cancer Mortality Reduction Act and various actions related to lung-cancer research, I received an invitation to apply for a lung-cancer advocacy summit through the National Lung Cancer Partnership in 2009. The partnership was in search of a limited number of survivors and caregivers to come to Dallas, Texas, to be trained on how to become effective grassroots advocates to increase lung-cancer awareness. I submitted my application in hopes that I would be among the chosen survivors.

I was overjoyed when I was accepted to participate in the summit. I was looking forward to finally being around like-minded people with the same goal. I needed direction to see how I could make a bigger impact with my advocacy efforts. Plus, I knew I would finally meet some other individuals who had been diagnosed with lung cancer who would be able to understand what I was going through.

The summit opened a whole new vision on advocacy for me. The training went through advocating through the media and newspaper to lobbying for laws to be passed. They even discussed ways to fund-raise for research. The partnership awards grants to lung-cancer researchers to support innovative research.

I was able to share my story with others in attendance at the summit and hear other stories of both survival and heartache from some of the caregivers. All of us had turned our frustrations and anger to a larger cause: to stand up against the dismal outlook for individuals diagnosed with lung cancer and fight. My mandate was from a higher calling, and I knew I was alive to give the disease a voice for all of those who had gone before me.

During the summit, we were also able to see firsthand innovative research being conducted in various areas of lung-cancer research. It was even more eye-opening to discover that there was even a disparity in the research among non–small-cell lung cancer and small-cell lung cancer. My hope was cut short and some anger reignited within me when I saw that only a limited amount of research was being conducted specifically for small-cell lung cancer.

I met another small-cell lung-cancer survivor at the summit who was devoted to improving lung-cancer research. I was moved by her boldness, commitment, and dedication to the lung-cancer community. Her vision was to establish a state chapter of the National Lung Cancer Partnership in Pennsylvania.

I also met a caregiver who reminded me of how important it was for me to give this disease a voice. I met a young woman who was representing her niece, who had died of small-cell lung cancer. One night as we were talking, I shared my life outside of cancer, sharing the small details that involved my career as a special-education teacher, my pursuit to complete my master's degree in special education, and my faith. Her eyes began to well up with tears as she looked at me and told me that her niece had been in school studying to be a special educator and that her middle name was also Marie. She gave me a bookmark and wristband to remember her niece. When I finished my master's degree, I wore the wristband and thought of her (I was living that moment for her as well). Again I knew my life was not my own.

Through the partnership, the doors for advocacy were opened wide, and a stronger passion burned within me as all of us left the summit with an individual plan of action. Through them, I have been able to spread my message through being featured in magazine articles, speaking at additional events, and participating in a work group to develop materials for other advocates and patients. I have also been able to participate on panels as a consumer advocate, reviewing research studies to rate the level of impact for lung-cancer patients.

When the doors of opportunity for advocacy opened, I had to listen to and meditate on the words of one of Donald Lawrence's songs entitled "Seasons". The lyrics discuss how it is time for the listeners to walk into their season.

At that moment, I knew all I had gone through was preparing me for this moment. The timing was right for me to come to the season of growth and an increased level of faith.

Since my diagnosis, I have been able to experience the simple joys of life with new eyes. Experiencing the graduation of my two youngest siblings and younger cousin from high school was something magical in itself. Until you know the opportunity to see your loved ones accomplish something great can be taken away in the twinkling of an eye, the significance of the moment can easily pass you by. Since my diagnosis, I have been able to see my second godchild come into this world in 2011, and I am enjoying seeing both of my godchildren grow and prosper.

I also met individuals through the lung-cancer summit who said they were fighting this disease and were going to continue to fight for their children. Their strength continues to inspire and encourage me.

When I was diagnosed with cancer, I had to take some time off from my graduate program and wondered if I would ever finish. After a semester off, I was able to return and achieved my master's degree. At one point I did know if I would be able to complete my degree because of my illness.

16

How Does One Survive?

Here is the test to try to find whether your mission on Earth is finished: If you're alive, it isn't.

—Richard Bach

God gave me a testimony so I could speak the words of His healing power with boldness, regardless of the place I was in or the crowd that was placed before me. I was invited to sit on a panel as a survivor at a lung-cancer educational seminar that involved telling the audience my personal experience with lung cancer. After the other panel member and I told our stories, audience members came up to the microphone to ask us questions. A gentleman stepped up to the microphone and asked with assurance, "I want to know from the experts: how does one survive lung cancer?"

I looked at the advocate next to me on the panel, and then I scanned the room, searching for the doctors who had spoken before us. Surely they were the experts this gentleman was referring to. Through the silence, I realized he was calling *us* the experts. Of course that made sense. *We* were the former patients; we were the only ones who could provide a first-person perspective to answer his question. I felt as if minutes were passing by in silence as neither the other panel member nor I responded. My mind was struggling with what to say. "This may be a secular setting. Do I tell them God healed me?" I wondered. I won the struggle in my head and decided to proclaim that my faith and my support from friends and family were how I had survived lung cancer. Funny thing, but the other panel member had a similar response.

Sometimes when I am asked questions about survival and making it through, I can feel the passion and pain of the individual. On one occasion, a young woman was asking me questions about how I had made it, and I told her I made it through by my faith. However, she still wanted to know *how* I was able to endure.

She told me about her sister's struggle and how she had stood by her sister during the journey. She gave a little bit of her cultural background (the audience I was talking to was composed of international students learning English) and explained with passion that no matter what she said or how she told her sister they would pray, her sister just seemed to give up and had lost hope. I had to tell her that the road was not always smooth and easy and that I did have down times and times when my faith was weak, but I had to hold on to the words spoken to me. For the patients, it is often hard for us to walk in the shoes of our caregivers, and the opposite is true as well.

If I had gone with the first doubt that crossed my head when asked "How does one survive?" I would have missed out on proclaiming my testimony for God's glory. Most assuredly, I can tell you how one survives lung cancer: One survives lung cancer by standing strong in the Lord and having faith in the words spoken in Isaiah: "But He was wounded for our transgressions, He was bruised for our iniquities; the chastisement for our peace was upon Him, and by His stripes, we are healed" (Isaiah 53:5). One survives by proclaiming, "But to you who fear My name, the Sun of Righteousness shall arise with healing in His wings; and you shall go out and grow fat like stall-fed calves" (Malachi 4:2). You survive by swallowing your pride, humbling yourself, and letting those God has placed in your life walk alongside you on the journey.

Survivors can seek rest for their weary souls by finding rest in the Lord: "Come to Me, all you who labor and are heavy laden, and I will give you rest. Take my yoke upon you and learn from Me, for

I am gentle and lowly in heart, and you will find rest for your souls. For My yoke is easy and My burden is light" (Matthew 11:28–30).

Several years ago as I started my journey of submitting my life to the Lord, my Aunt Andrea gave me a study Bible as a gift. When she presented the Bible to me, she shared a scripture that was meaningful in her life, Psalm 139. Psalm 139 speaks of God's perfect knowledge of man. In verses 5–10, my eyes were opened to God's sovereignty over our lives:

> You have hedged me behind and before, and laid your hand before me. Such knowledge is too wonderful for me; it is high, I cannot attain it. Where can I go from Your spirit? Or where can I flee from Your presence? If I ascend into heaven, You are there; if I make my bed in hell, behold, You are there. If I take the wings of the morning, and dwell in the uttermost parts of the sea, even there Your hand shall lead me, and Your right hand shall hold me.

The Lord was with me through every step of this journey and in every step of my life. There was nowhere I could go that He was not there. He was with me in my grandmother's passing, when I went through my divorce, and as I faced cancer. He was with me through radiation, surgery, and chemotherapy. It is so awesome that God is everywhere. He knows all, and He made us; therefore, He knows us. One survives by understanding God's sovereignty over our lives.

I survived by seeking help from others and not letting worry overwhelm me. When this journey started and I realized I could not endure dealing with medical-insurance concerns or scheduling appointments, I turned them over to my Aunt Deborah, who by profession had experience scheduling patients and dealing with insurance companies. With open arms, I accepted the gifts of prepared food from family and friends. What could worrying add to my situation? "Therefore do not worry about tomorrow, for tomorrow will worry about its own things. Sufficient for the day is its own trouble" (Matthew 6:34).

My family and friends walked this journey with me. There were times when I was down and answered the phone to a person delivering the words I needed to hear in that moment to get me over the hump. Thank God that members of my church family stepped up and volunteered their time to sit with me through chemotherapy treatments, drive me to my treatments, and lift up my name before the Father in prayer. Cards and gifts would spontaneously greet me through the mail. Some of my best friends whom I had known since childhood were scattered in various locations, but they still continued to call, send me text messages, and pray. To them, I am eternally grateful.

In addition, I continued to survive by taking a stand against lung cancer and using my life and voice to open eyes about this deadly disease. An eternal flame has been ignited deep within me to spread this testimony wherever I go, bring a voice to this silent killer, and tell my miraculous story of healing. My life is not my own, and my being here five years later did not come from "luck" or from my own strength. I am surviving and will continue to survive by living my life on purpose. Prayerfully, my life is being used to give life, hope, and inspiration to someone beyond myself through spreading this testimony of God's healing power.

17

From Survivor to Overcomer

When we do face the difficult times, we need to remember that circumstances don't make the person, they reveal a person.

—Emma Jameson

One day a coworker was challenging me to slow down and take a break in regards to basically being a workaholic, which led to a discussion on being in survival mode for an eternity. He stressed the fact that there had to be a time when I came out of just living every day of my life like I was in survival mode, just fighting to make it through. A dear friend challenged me with Scripture to change my definition of myself from *survivor* to *overcomer*.

If you look up the word *survive*, the definition states that it means "to remain alive, or in existence." I realized I was operating in a state of existence—existing at work, perhaps trying to reclaim the time I felt had slipped through my hands. I existed in my relationships with others, defining their actions by my insecurities and my long absence from social outings, while building a barricade around myself to protect me from venturing out to meet new people. You see, secretly I was wondering who had the potential to stay around during the difficult times of my life.

To me, to exist was good; it meant surviving, and it meant the miracle had come true. However, many things *exist* here on earth. The plants exist, the stars exist, and the houses we live in exist, but we are called to a higher definition. Amazingly, if you search for the word *survive* in the King James Version of the Bible, your results will yield zero.

According to *Merriam-Webster's Collegiate Dictionary*, the word *overcome* means "to get the better of: to surmount." Others define overcoming as defeating an opponent, prevailing. I am so grateful that my friend challenged me to look at the way I was defining myself. As the poem at the beginning of this book states, "Cancer is so limited." I turned to the Word of God to let the truth set in—that I was an overcomer.

During my journey, I stood on Revelation 12:11: "And they overcame him by the blood of the Lamb and by the word of their testimony." When a war raged in heaven between Michael and his angels against the devil and his angels, the servants of God prevailed and won the war. Since we are children of God, we have already won the battle.

Time and time again, God speaks words of victory for those who are in Christ:

- Overcoming the spirit of the Antichrist, who sends false prophets:
  "You are of God, little children, and have *overcome* them, because He who is in you is greater than he who is in the world" (1 John 4:4, emphasis added).
- Caleb telling the crowd of people they were capable of overcoming the Amalekites and possessing the land:
  "Then Caleb quieted the people before Moses, and said, 'Let us go up at once and take possession, for we are well able to *overcome* it'" (Numbers 13:30, emphasis added).
- Jesus assuring us that although we may have tribulations in the world, He has overcome the world:
  "These things I have spoken to you, that in Me you may have peace. In the world you will have tribulation; but be

of good cheer, I have *overcome* the world" (John 16:33, emphasis added).

- John addressing generations of believers:
  "I write to you, fathers, because you have known Him who is from the beginning. I write to you, young men, because you have *overcome* the wicked one. I write to you, little children, because you have known the Father. I have written to you, fathers, because you have known Him who is from the beginning. I have written to you, young men, because you are strong, and the word abides in you, and you have *overcome* the wicked one" (1 John 2:13–14, emphasis added).

The Lord has promised us that we have the victory because He is with us: "For in Him we live and move and have our being, as also some of your own poets have said, 'For we are also His offspring'" (Acts 17:28). After years of just surviving, I found freedom by getting hold of this concept.

The cancer was limited, but it helped shape my character into the person I am today. My testimony would prevail to impact the life of someone beyond myself. Therefore, defining myself as a "cancer survivor" had to change.

18

Overcomers

And they overcame him by the blood of the lamb
and by the word of their testimony.

—Revelation 12:11

Through this journey we call life, we often encounter trials and tribulations that shake us to the core. The fight-or-flight instinct kicks in and we begin to "survive." We survive a cancer diagnosis, the grief of losing a loved one, or a horrible accident; or we merely survive day-to-day life. I challenged a few of my friends to contribute their stories of overcoming. I pray that their testimonies bless you:

Terri Young, diagnosed with blood clots in both the lungs and legs:

I am a child of God, who blessed me with yet another chance. The reason I say this is because the first night I was in the hospital, I told God that if He called me home, I was okay with that. I felt that I had touched one person, and I was good with spending eternity with Him. I also asked Him to take care of my mom if He did call me home.

The conversation continued. If He didn't call me home, I was going to live my life differently. Since then, I can honestly say that I have made changes in my life and am growing in my relationship with God.

This experience showed me who God is. It helped me to see that there is power in prayer. My illness started a prayer chain that went from the East Coast to the West Coast and places in between. The last thing—and the hardest thing to swallow—was that there are consequences for decisions we make if they are not in line with what God has for us. I still have health issues that stem from this experience, but the fact that I am still here is enough for me to keep going, to keep chasing after God, to walk in the path that He has for me.

Bettina Hodges, daughter diagnosed with leukemia at the age of six months old and passed away at the age of twenty-one months:

I am an overcomer, a woman of faith and a woman who perseveres using God's Word. One of the scriptures I lived by and meditated on while caring for my daughter and that I still love is Romans 8:28: "All things work together for good to those who love God, to those who are the called according to His purpose."

Michelle Deese Brown, overcomer of pregnancy loss:

"Is that all you want?" the waitress asked, sounding mildly annoyed. She reminded me of Flo from the seventies TV sitcom *Alice*.

"Yes, that's it. Thank you." I was a thirty-five-year-old woman who felt no need to explain herself, even if the waitress couldn't quite tell that I was pregnant. The plate full of home fries was all I needed for momentary fulfillment.

People used to say that I looked like I had just had a big lunch. I was halfway through my pregnancy and still no one would give up their seat for me on the Metro. It was like a little secret. I wanted to blurt it out as soon as the doors chimed: "I'm pregnant! Can I get a seat?" I didn't. I would have looked foolish.

My OB/GYN teased my walk. "You're barely showing. Why are you waddling like that?" She thought I was doing a duck impression. "Just wait until you get really big. Then you'll have something to waddle about," she laughed.

She cried when I delivered a stillborn. It wasn't like we didn't already know my baby would be born silent. (That's what the grief counseling books I read called it—"born silent.") We were just shy of full-term—thirty-six weeks and six days—and when my contractions weren't regular, my doctor met me at the hospital, only to find no fetal heartbeat. The room was eerily quiet during delivery, save for my doctor's weeping.

The next day, while I held my tiny baby girl, the hospital chaplain came to visit us and performed a very nice naming ceremony for Mikaela.

It rained the day we left the hospital. It rained hard. For some reason, the nursing staff insisted that I be wheeled out to the lobby, although I could walk just fine. I sat in that wheelchair, unable to distinguish the rain from my tears, while my dead baby's father went to get the car. It was a scene from a movie—a very pathetic, poorly written story with a terrible ending and a miserable soundtrack.

Even after five years, memories from that time in the hospital are vivid. That feeling of heavy yet empty arms was unlike any helpless feeling I've ever experienced.

"Why me, God? Other people have sinned worse than me. Why am I being punished and not them?" I asked. The movie's story line quickly turned from sadness and grief to anger and disbelief. I couldn't understand why I was being blacklisted from the "mommy club" when I had so desperately wanted in all my life. Why were some women granted children they didn't want or couldn't properly care for? "It's not fair" became my daily mantra.

Was it the abortion I had had in college? Was it the premarital sex I regularly engaged in? Surely God couldn't be punishing me for that stuff. I knew I wasn't living right, but give me a break. I wasn't a bad person. What could I have done that would warrant such cruel punishment?

The only real answer I received to my questions was that God is sovereign. No one actually said it to me. It appeared softly in my spirit at some point out of nowhere. I had heard the word *sovereign* in church for years yet didn't really know what it meant. What I did know for certain was that my control-freak nature had gotten up and exited stage left. That could have been the end. Instead, it was a beginning.

For several months afterwards, everything I knew was questioned. I could say nothing with absolute certainty. At first, I wondered what good it did to make plans when God could change the course, literally in a heartbeat. It reminded me of when older people said they would do this or that, "God willing." Now I knew the wisdom in that saying.

Overcoming doesn't mean forgetting or denying my daughter's existence. I still often wonder about Mikaela's untold story as I watch my three-year-old romp with an abundance of life and energy. What it does mean is that I focus more on what's important and let the small things slide. I listen more to my inner spirit, allowing myself to be guided in the right direction. I'm much more patient and contemplative, self-aware almost to a fault.

Losing my baby mostly taught me to give everything over to God—everything.

Scriptures for Healing

Use the scriptures below to learn what the Bible tells us about healing. Personalize these scriptures and meditate on them, having faith and hope.

- "Have mercy on me, O Lord, for I am weak; O Lord, heal me, for my bones are troubled" (Psalm 6:2).
- "O Lord my God, I cried out to You, and You healed me" (Psalm 30:2).
- "Bless the Lord, O my soul; and all that is within me, bless His holy name! Bless the Lord, O my soul, and forget not his all His benefits: who forgives all your iniquities, who heals all your diseases, who redeems your life from destruction, who crowns you with lovingkindness and tender mercies" (Psalm 103:1–4).
- "He sent His word and healed them, and delivered them from their destructions" (Psalm 107:20).

- "My son, give attention to my words; incline your ear to my sayings. Do not let them depart from your eyes; keep them in the midst of your heart; for they are life to those who find them, and health to all their flesh. Keep your heart with all diligence, for out of it spring the issues of life" (Proverbs 4:20–23).
- "But He was wounded for our transgressions, He was bruised for our iniquities; the chastisement for our peace was upon Him, and by His stripes we are healed" (Isaiah 53:5).
- "Then your light shall break forth like the morning, your healing shall spring forth speedily, and your righteousness shall go before you; the glory of the Lord shall be your rear guard" (Isaiah 58:8).
- "Heal me, O Lord, and I shall be healed; save me, and I shall be saved, for You are my praise" (Jeremiah 17:14).
- "'For I will restore health to you and heal you of your wounds,' says the Lord, 'because they called you an outcast saying: "This is Zion; no one seeks her"'" (Jeremiah 30:17).
- "But to you who fear My name the Sun of Righteousness shall arise with healing in His wings; and you shall go out and grow fat like stall-fed calves" (Malachi 4:2).

- "And He said to her, 'Daughter, be of good cheer, your faith has made you well. Go in peace'" (Luke 8:48).
- "And it happened that the father of Publius lay sick of a fever and dysentery. Paul went in to him and prayed, and he laid his hands on him and healed him. So when this was done, the rest of those on the island who had diseases also came and were healed" (Acts 28:8–9).
- "Beloved, I pray that you may prosper in all things and be in health, just as your soul prospers" (3 John 2).

Jesus performed several miracles during His earthly ministry. Many of them included miraculous healings of restoring sight to the blind and causing the mute to speak. Listed below are accounts of healings recorded in the New Testament:

- "And Jesus went about Galilee, teaching in their synagogues, preaching the gospel of the kingdom, and healing all kinds of sickness and all kinds of disease among the people" (Matthew 4:23).
- In Mark 8:22–26, we find the account of Jesus healing a blind man in Bethsaida.
- Mark 10:46–52 tells the story of a blind man named Bartimaeus. After he pleaded with Jesus to have mercy

on him, Jesus summoned him and asked what He could do for him. When he requested that he wished to receive his sight, Jesus answered, "'Go your way; your faith has made you well.' And immediately he received his sight and followed Jesus on the road" (Mark 10:52).

- Jesus healed a man who was blind from birth by making clay, anointing the man's eyes with it, and telling him to wash the clay off in John 9:1–12.
- Individuals with leprosy in biblical times were the outcasts of society. They lived their lives in a level of isolation mandated by the laws of the day to maintain specific measurements of distance between them and "normal" people, yet Jesus was willing to heal them. In Luke 5:12–16, a man full of leprosy was healed immediately. In Luke 17:11–19, Jesus healed ten lepers.

Lung-Cancer Advocacy Organizations and Initiatives

- Chris Draft Family Foundation—Team Draft

  www.teamdraft.org
- Free to Breathe

  www.freetobreathe.org
- Lung Cancer Action Network—LungCAN

  www.lungcan.org
- Lung Cancer Alliance

  www.lungcanceralliance.org
- LUNGevity

  www.lungevity.org

To Be Continued . . .

Two roads diverged in a wood, and I—I took the road less traveled by, and that has made all the difference.

—Robert Frost

January 29, 2012

Dear Father,

Thank You for Your grace and mercy. Thank You for the power of healing. Lord, when I said yes to Your will and Your way and committed my life to follow You, I never imagined what that would involve, but You have shown me that through You all things are possible.

I started writing this story You gave me years ago, but I set it aside because I clearly needed to hear Your will and build a level of confidence to step out in faith. Thank You for clearly using Your child Matthew to speak the words I needed to hear to proceed and have confidence to finish what I had started.

As my five-year anniversary date for my diagnosis came and went on December 21, 2011, a passion was reignited within me to remind me that I was living above and beyond the statistics because of Your healing power. As I told Dr. McKnight, I was going to be his miracle case. Thank You for using this kind, gentle man who never gave me a time limit for my life and always asked me how I was doing through this journey.

Thank You for whispering those words of life to me before I knew for sure what the diagnosis was. Thank You for surrounding me with loving and caring friends and family who not only helped my physical needs, but also lifted me up in prayer and encouragement. As this journey continues, please continue to use my life for Your will and help my testimony be a light for someone beyond myself. I pray that these words will encourage and inspire someone.

Lord, I continue to lift up all the names of those who are fighting cancer. Let them be strong and courageous through this battle. Remind them that by Your stripes, they are healed! Give them and their loved ones a peace that surpasses all understanding.

In Your service,

Montessa M. Lee

But as it is written: "Eye has not seen, nor ear heard, nor have entered into the heart of man the things which God has prepared for those who love Him."

—1 Corinthians 2:9

From left: Maya, me and Chaunelle

Katja with her husband

Here I am with my
Dr. John McKnight.

Attending a *Survivor at Every Arena* event with friends, another lung cancer survivor, an oncologist and my support team sponsored by *Team Draft*: Chris Draft is second from the right and I am third from the right.

Here I am at my graduation from Johns Hopkins University with my parents.

This picture was taken on my second mission trip to Trelawny, Jamaica after my lung cancer diagnosis. I am first from the right.

Terri Young

Bettina Hodges

Michelle Deese Brown

CPSIA information can be obtained at www.ICGtesting.com
Printed in the USA
LVOW01s1524310715

448273LV00002B/2/P

9 781498 441643